How To Go Up in a Down Economy

......and have fun doing it.

Lawrence Surles

authorHOUSE®

AuthorHouse™
1663 Liberty Drive
Bloomington, IN 47403
www.authorhouse.com
Phone: 1-800-839-8640

First published by AuthorHouse   5/26/2009

ISBN: 978-1-4389-6592-5 (sc)

Printed in the United States of America
Bloomington, Indiana

This book is printed on acid-free paper.

Disclaimer: This book, as all our materials are designed to provide accurate information regarding the subject matter covered. This material is not intended to replace legal qualified advice. There are no warranties, expressed or implied as to the performance of presented materials. We provide all materials as an educational service. Each reader should use his own judgment of the applicability of any of the presented techniques, ideals, recommendations, and suggestions.

ACKNOWLEDGEMENTS

I acknowledge God Jehovah as being the Lord of my life. I am thankful for his son Jesus, who died on the cross for the redemption of my sins. I accept the fact that he freed me from the curse of the Law of Moses. I understand there is nothing I can do that will cause him to love me more than he already does. I thank him for making a new creation of me, and renewing a righteous spirit in me day by day.

I would like to thank my lovely wife, Bettie, for being supportive of my efforts. Many thanks go out to my son, Lawrence Surles II, and his wife Clarice, for their input in this project.

I say thank you to my mother, Clory W. Surles, who has gone on to be with the Lord. Also, thanks to my mother-in-law, Rosa B. Johnson, who also have gone on to be with God, for allowing her daughter to be my wife. To all my sisters, brothers, cousins, nieces and nephews; especially William and Christian Crockett. I love you all!

I also acknowledge my cousin, Calvin Wills, who never hesitates to offer his assistance in any way that he can. Also, to Quinyelle Hicks, thank you for your help.

I acknowledge my co-workers at Wal-Mart Incorporated because they have been such a fun group of people to work with. I thank them for giving me the opportunity to grow spiritually and socially.

About This Book

The bad news!

This book is not about how to get rich quick. It is definitely not about spending your life accumulating objects that will only turn to dust.

The good news!

This book takes a back-to-basics approach. It's about living well-for-less. It's about living from the inside-out. Within these pages it makes every effort to present materials in an easy-to-understand format. It is for everyday people who feel the need to live a more meaningful life that reflects their true potential. Never does it make any unrealistic claims to give a cure-all-solution to life's problems. Neither, does it imply that you can improve your life without putting forth honest and committed efforts.

Our objective is to stimulate your mind, give you access to simple down-to-earth strategies that can help you to wake up, get up, go up, and stay up in any type of economy. Simply put, our aim is to help you "spend less than you earn and enjoy it".

More about This Book - A Real Estate Broker

Being a real estate broker for the past 13 yrs, I can truly see your vision and where this book is leading this next generation. The message in your book is so clear, and the life that you are living has inspired me and many of my close associates to step it up a notch in the way we handle our everyday finances. You demonstrated so clearly in your book , many of the key fundamentals to getting out of debt, a simple written plan of instructions that's easy to follow, and once you've built the wealth; how to keep it! Parents, I recommend you buy this book for your children before puberty. It's like putting money in the bank for your future.

Ruben Surles
Real Estate Broker
San Antonio, Texas

About the Author

He was born March 1953 in Linden, NC. He has a total of more than 23 years of military experience. His business experience spans over 34 years in business and corporate management; including twelve years in a thriving home-based communications business. He is a Christian, and attributes his success to the one and only living God. Mr. Surles started his writing career in 2002 while working at a major retailer. He felt the need to share his experiences that could enhance the lives of others.

Table of Contents

Introduction

Why am I writing this book? Because I know that the majority of Americans are in debt, or living paycheck to paycheck; and our government is in worst shape. In a nation where we often refuse to spend less that what we earn; we tend to judge our success by the number of things we possess. Too long we have tried to satisfy our petty wants, while sacrificing a more prosperous future for ourselves.

I personally know many people that are suffering, as I did, from the pain and embarrassment of over spending. I see the desperation from folks trying to figure out a way to deal with the rising costs of energy, and still maintain a healthy lifestyle. I'm convinced that we can do well in today's economy. Sometimes it takes a crisis to awaken us from our slumber of complacency. Within these pages, I offer you opportunities to make informed decisions, not cheap choices. That is great news in a time when we seem to be working harder to bring home less.

The interest on debts is bleeding this country dry, and our economy is in serious trouble. We need to be proactive in selecting real leaders that don't put the chase of fame and fortune before the people they serve. Real leaders who rarely have to declare their authority, but those that lead by the example, the caliber of their work, personal conduct, and personal performance that really speak the real truth about their motives. This is the time when the accomplishments of the people they serve will indicate the real success of their leaders.

In this book, I seek to turn your focus toward building positive, win-win, relationships. I teach that you need to be grateful for what you do have, and be more willing to share what you have with others in need. We believe that greater opportunities are available to people who make the most of small ones that come their way.

This book offers you an opportunity to be a participant, not just a spectator in life. We challenge you not to hide behind myths and excuses that cause most of us to live within the opinions of others. We can excel, if we believe it, one person at time.

CHAPTER ONE
PREPARE A WRITTEN ASSESSMENT
OF YOUR SITUATION

Chapter One Objectives: This chapter will help you analyze your current situation, potential problems, and allow you to find out what is the root cause of your problems. This information will allow you to better understand what you need to do to solve many issues that confront you. By the end of this chapter, you should be able to evaluate where you are in relation to the goals that you wish to accomplish.

A WORD FOR THE WISE - Acknowledge you have a problem

Stop and take an honest look at your life's situation. If you would be totally honest with yourself, you would have to admit that you've accomplished only a fraction of the dreams you envisioned after high school.

If you are one of those people who face a tremendous financial challenge, you tend to go into denial. In other words, you won't admit that you have a real problem. It can be very embarrassing to admit you're skating on thin ice. If you are barely getting the bills paid, and still feel like you are still going around in circles, going nowhere fast, then you are reading the right book. Deep in your heart, you may not see any chance of improvement in your lifestyle, but rest assured that real change comes from within. Nothing will improve by magic, or by bribing God, thinking you can force him to perform a miracle on your behalf.

But, there is good news! Instead of "throwing in the towel", and settling for living far below the true potential that God has given to you, just admit that life's problems are too big for you to handle alone. This is actually the first and most important step in becoming a truly free new creation, capable of doing all things through Christ Jesus.

What's your current situation?

Your financial budget situation will fit in one of these categories. There will be times when you will slide from one category to another. These categories are as follows:

1. **You have a positive cash flow:** You have money left over after you pay your bills.
2. **You are at break even:** You barely have enough money to cover your bills.
3. **You have a negative cash flow:** Your expenses are greater than your income. Simply put, you are spending more than you earn. This includes borrowing from your friends and regular withdrawals from your savings or other accounts. Before you know it, your friends won't lend you any more money, and your savings and checking accounts will be almost empty. If your credit card is close to being maxed out, it's also a sign that you may be spending more than you earn.

Let's Get Started

You will need to purchase a calendar that includes daily, weekly, and monthly scheduling. Preferably, a note book size scheduler that you can carry with you daily, in which to write in other tasks you wish to schedule. These are some of the examples that you may want to consider as you schedule events in your planning calendar.

- If you are married, record the birthday, and anniversary of your mate.
- Record the birthdays and anniversaries of others you wish to remember.
- Record other special days and events such as cookouts, family reunions, etc.
- Remember to schedule family time and time for yourself.

Continue gathering the information that you may need to help you reach desired goals in life. Make a habit of spending at least 30-45 minutes a week working on this project. You may choose to make a lose leaf organizer or folder in which to store all related materials. If you choose to utilize your computer for this task instead, this is perfectly ok.

If you are married, it is important that you create your budget and planning together. You will have a better chance of reaching your goals when you harness the power of teamwork.

Once you've settled on a plan, take a minute to start writing your plans on paper, or use your computer if you have budgeting or planning software available. Research shows that people who write down, and monitor their goals are more likely to accomplish them.

In order to assess your current situation, you must identify your current mental, spiritual, and physical conditions. This is necessary in order to assess where you are now in relation to where you desire to be. As you continue planning, you should consider some of the following in your assessments: How much do you own? How much do you earn? How much do you spend? Is the difference of what you earn and spend, negative or positive? How many people are dependent on you for income and support? Are you beginning to the idea?

What is debt?

An amount or value due to someone that is to be paid back in the future, in most cases from future earnings. You normally incur debt because you want the use of something before payment is paid in full. In almost every case the price of things purchased this way costs more.

What are some of the negative effects, feelings, or problems that your debt or bills maybe causing?   True / False

1.	_____	I don't have increased stress in your life.
2.	_____	I don't feel that I are a failure in life.
3.	_____	I don't have embarrassment and disgrace because of the debt you owe.
4.	_____	I tend not to worry about how bills are going to be paid.
5.	_____	I tend to have higher than normal auto or home insurance premiums.
6.	_____	My bad credit doesn't prohibit employment in certain jobs.
7.	_____	I have to put deposits on new utilities or cell phone contracts.
8.	_____	I do not pay high interest on loans (9% or more).
9.	_____	I do not to get calls or letters from debt collectors.

*Give yourself 1 point for each statement you answer true to. Record the total points earned.*_____

Negative Statistics and Concerns that affect your debts and credit situation

- More than 2/3 of USA families are living paycheck to paycheck.
- Most bankruptcies could have been avoided if those individuals could have earned at least $300 extra a month.
- Over 50% of Americans have no retirement savings.
- 20 -30% of the income of financial institutions come from late fees, over- the limit -charges, and default rates.
- Energy costs are rising faster than the median income.
- Inflation is out-pacing wage increases.
- Personal and business bankruptcies are increasing.
- US trade deficits are on the increase and bank failures are looming.
- Lay offs and down-sizing.
- Sub-prime housing defaults.
- Government bailouts threaten higher tax burdens.
- Retirement plan losses.
- Government debt on the rise.

You can earn a fortune in your lifetime!

The totals below represent your average income earned a year for 40 years of work, and the amount you could expect to earn in a lifetime.

Amount you earn per year	Total lifetime earnings
$ 25,000	$1,000,000
50,000	2,000,000
75,000	3,000,000

*It's not just what you earn that counts, it's what you are able to keep, and what you build with what you keep.

Personal Profile Assessment

- Married/Single/Divorced –Circle one.
- Date I started reading this book. Date _____
- I work <u>fulltime</u> or <u>part-time</u>. Circle one.
- Male or Female –Circle one.
- I have _____ dependents.
- I am a US citizen or is authorized to work in the USA. _____ yes/ no
- Years of Education completed _____
- I am working a second job. Yes _____ No _____
- Occupation (s) 1._____ 2._____
- Additional Skills 1 _____ 2. _____
  3._____
  4._____

- I feel that I am in fair / good / great health / for my age. Circle one.
- The highest amount of total debt I would be comfortable with having is $ _____.
- I would like to take _____ vacations a year (How many?).
- How many people live in your home? _____.
- How many wage earners live in your home? _____.
- My financial plan does include having or raising children. _____ yes/no
- I have filed for bankruptcy in the past ten years _____ yes/no
- I have been refused a bond in the last 5 years. _____ yes/no
- I have whole life insurance. _____ yes/ no
- I have term life insurance. _____ yes / no
- My insurance accumulates cash value. _____ yes / no
- I normally get a large tax refund _____ yes / no
- I normally get a small tax refund. _____ yes / no
- I feel my current financial plan will allow me to retire at the financial level I desire. _____ yes/ no
- I don't have a job. _____ yes / no
- I would like to retire at age _____.
- I have made plans to pay for my children's education. _____ yes / no
- Do you think each partner should have a personal fund to buy the things that they want or need? _____ yes/ no _____
- I owe child support. yes/no _____
- I watch at least _____ hours of TV per day.
- If you could give yourself a raise, how much would it be? _____ .
- A saving account is important to me. _____.yes / no.
- My favorite magazine is _____.
- Name several things I would like to learn from this book.

Survey: Assessment of how you see yourself

True /False

A. _____ I take responsibility for my actions.
B. _____ I am resourceful.
C. _____ I try to get the best use of things and situations.
D. _____ I make efforts to understand the view points of others.
E. _____ I make an effort to understand myself and why I do what I do.
F. _____ I make a reasonable effort to be friendly to others.
G. _____ I am honest.

Give yourself 1 point for each true response. Points earned _____.

These are reasons why you may want to be financially stable.

- Freedom to give generously at church and to your favorite charity.
- College education for your kids.
- No need to work overtime because you have to.
- Take a nice vacation, or travel often.
- Retire while you are young and healthy enough to enjoy it.
- Better home or automobile.
- Pay off student loans and other debts.
- Start the business you always wanted.
- Pay off your home or purchase a new one.
- Set up a trust for future generations.
- Enjoy better control of how you spend your time.
- You believe it would not be possible to maintain your present lifestyle on social security income alone.
- You dislike the stress of living paycheck to paycheck.
- You don't want to be a burden and depend on your relatives to help you pay bills when you retire or become disabled.

Some potential causes of debt

- Medical expenses
- Job loss
- Divorce/separation
- Poor management skills, poor problem solving skills (lack of organization)
- Economic changes
- Unclear and unbraided spending priorities
- Gambling, greed
- Inherited debts
- Lack of knowledge
- Under-earning and no regular saving plan
- Pride

Recognizing some of the warning signs that you have debt overload or potential credit challenges:

1. You have three or more credit cards.
2. You write postdated checks.
3. You have made little or no preparation for retirement other than social security income.
4. You have no residual income.
5. You frequently receive late charges or "over-the-limit charges."
6. You hold payment on one bill to pay another (juggling).
7. You think negatively about your debts often.
8. You use "pay day lending" companies for borrowing.

9. You regularly hide debts from your spouse.
10. You are too embarrassed to talk about how much you owe?
11. You are nearing the limits on _any_ of your credit cards.
12. You can't pay the bills if your spouse does not work.
13. You do not save a portion of your income regularly.
14. You normally borrow money to go on a vacation.
15. You have been denied credit.
16. You aren't able to pay your credit card balance in full when it comes.
17. You are only able to pay the minimum amount due on your credit card.
18. You have to work two or more jobs to make ends meet.
19. You pay high interest loans.
20. You have to pay deposits on utilities.
21. You co-signed for loans that you can't afford to pay back.
22. You have heated discussions about money with your spouse.

General Assessment Survey-True/False

Note: The assessment questions or statements below will have reference to your situations or actions within the last 12 months, unless otherwise indicated.

1. _____ I do not spend more than I earn.
2. _____ I have two or less personal credit cards.
3. _____ I am not nearing the credit limit on any of my credit cards (I owe 50% or more of my credit card limit).
4. _____ I did not write a postdated check in the last 12 months.
5. _____ I don't think sad thoughts often about my debts.
6. _____ I did not use "pay day lending" companies to borrow money in the last 12 months.
7. _____ I do not have debts on which I don't make payments.
8. _____ Most of the time my paycheck covers my all bills.
9. _____ I saved a portion of my last paycheck.
10. _____ If my spouse lost their income, I could still pay the bills.
11. _____ I have a valid will in force.
12. _____ I have at least $500 in liquid savings.
13. _____ I have at least $1,000 in liquid savings.
14. _____ I do not owe property taxes from last year.
15. _____ I did not borrow money for a vacation in the last 12 months.
16. _____ I did not pay late fees within the last 12 months.
17. _____ I have a savings account.
18. _____ I did not bounce a check or have an overdraft in the last 12 months.
19. _____ I have health insurance.
20. _____ I have enough life insurance to cover my debts and final expenses.
21. _____ I have a job, or other reliable income.
22. _____ I did not get a call or letter from a creditor in the last 12 months.
23. _____ I balance my checking account at least monthly.

24.	_____	If I were to take a vacation, I will not have to borrow money. .
25.	_____	I buy ahead when I see food and household items go on sale.
26.	_____	I have at least one certificate of deposit (CD).
27.	_____	I have more than one source of income.
28.	_____	I have made arrangements how my final expenses will be paid.
29.	_____	When I retire I don't expect to live on my social security income alone.
30.	_____	I owe less than 20% of what I own.
31.	_____	I didn't have a returned check within the last 12 months.
32.	_____	My total credit balances have not increased.
33.	_____	I did not juggle any of my bills in the last 12 months (I skipped a bill to pay another).
34.	_____	I do not have to work overtime in order to pay my bills.
35.	_____	I know how much my total debts are.
36.	_____	I have not used my credit card to buy necessities like food and gas, because I did not have the money.
37.	_____	I don't hide my purchases from my spouse.
38.	_____	I am buying my home.
39.	_____	I don't owe a balance on my home.
40.	_____	I don't have a 2nd or 3rd mortgage on my home.
41.	_____	I am not too embarrassed to ask for help.
42.	_____	I didn't skip a payment offered by my credit card company.
43.	_____	I have a job, or other reliable income.
44.	_____	I know how much I earn each month.
45.	_____	I know the total value of what I own (assets).
46.	_____	I spend at least 30 minutes a month reading a book or magazine.
47.	_____	I usually do not carry large amounts of cash in my wallet or purse.
48.	_____	I don't hold on to convenience checks in case I need extra money.

Give yourself 1 point for each true response. Points earned. _____.

Look for patterns of spending that could indicate trouble

There's no magic number of statements with which you must agree to determine if you have a credit problem. Everyone's situation is unique. If you had to pawn an item to make ends meet several times in the last 12 months, this is a sign of trouble. Likewise, paying of minimum amounts due once in a while could be acceptable. But, if you notice a continual increase in credit balances, you may be headed for real trouble. Also, if you see that your savings account balance is decreasing fast because your paycheck has been running short, this could be another indicator of serious trouble ahead. But, we hope that you will be able to "True" to all the survey quiz statements in each chapter.

Don't wait too long –Don't be afraid to ask for help

Getting help sooner, can take months or years off the process of getting out of debt, or to eliminate the stress of paycheck to paycheck living. Don't wait until you've hit rock bottom financially! If you do, it will take years longer to work your way out of debt, or paycheck to paycheck living. Don't procrastinate any longer; there are many non-profit credit counseling agencies that are available to help you. Seeking credit counseling before things get too far out of hand eases the stress of financial burdens on families.

In this book, many times, getting your affairs organized so you can make an accurate assessment of your situation may be all the help you need. It is my intentions to share timely tips gained from my years of experience in this journey called life.

Make a list of things you wanted to accomplish when you were in the 12th grade, or your last year in school.

If you feel it is still possible to attain any of these goals, write them along with short, midterm, and long term goals in this chapter.

List eight (8) key things you would like to accomplish with the remainder of your life.

	Year
	Year
	Year
	Year
	Year
	Year
	Year
	Year

List these in your short, midterm, or long term goals in chapter 3 and 4. Give yourself one point for each accomplishment you have completed. Points earned _____.

List some of your bad habits:

List these in your short, midterm, or long term goals. Feel free to use the CHECKLIST TO HELP YOU SOLVE BAD HABITS or other issues below.

Your Checklist to Problem Solving

Please only list one issue or situation per page. You can make as many copies of this page as you need.

- Step 1- Identify and clarify the problem.
- Step 2- Gather as much information as possible.
- Step 3- Evaluate the evidence you have collected.
- Step 4- Consider the alternatives, pros and cons of any actions you may take.
- Step 5- Choose and implement the best alternatives.
- Step 6- Review, evaluate, and revise your actions regularly.

Your problem, issue, situation, or bad habit is:

_____

List as many suggestions that you think may be able to help correct, or reduce the impact of the bad habits or issue that you listed above. Please include the pros and cons of each suggestion:

Please line through each suggestion as you accomplish it.
This issue or habit has been solved to my satisfaction. Circle one: Yes / No

List five (5) things you believe are holding you back in life. (Example: Bad credit, bad temper).

What are your strengths? (These are your best talents, skills, and personality traits).

What are your weaknesses? (These are things that you need to improve upon.)

Below, list ways you might seek to improve each of your weaknesses.

List these in your short, midterm, or long term goals

My List of Things to Do

Make your list in the order of importance, or by the date you expect to accomplish it. If you can't accomplish them in the next 30 days, then take them off this list, and transfer them to your short, medium, or long term budget goals list. **List only things you plan to do in the next 30 days. Make 12 copies of this sheet, one for each month.**

Date you would like to complete this goal	Description of your goal

My short term budget goals are: (On a sheet of paper list the things you would to complete within the next 31 days to12 months): List the month you would like to have each item completed beside each entry. On the second line, explain why each is important to you. Some examples are: new job, marriage, new washer, new dryer, repairs, etc. *Draw a line through each item as you accomplish it, or you may replace it with another goal you wish to accomplish.*

Goal Description	Month

List your mid-term budget goals (List things you would like to complete starting at one year to five years). Please list as many additional lines as you need. *Draw a line through each item as you accomplish it. You may wish to add other things to this list.*

Goal Description	Month/ Year

List your Long-term budget goals (Things you would like to complete within five years and beyond). List things you would like to accomplish within this period of time. Please list as many additional lines as you need. *Draw a line through each item as you accomplish it.*

Goal Description	Month/Year

Let's take another step - Establish a budget to help you reach your goals

Just when you thought you would have a few extra dollars, something seems to always happen. Do you ever stop and wonder where your money goes each month? Does it seem like you're never able to get ahead? Before you know it, you are out of money, and the month is not over yet. If so, you may want to establish a budget to help you keep track of how you spend your money and help you reach your financial goals. We have prepared a sample budget in this book.

Examine your financial goals

Before you establish a budget, you should determine what your financial goals are. Start by making a list of your short-term goals, midterm, and long-term goals; such as the one you just completed in this chapter. Next, ask yourself, why is it important for me to achieve this goal? How much will I need to save to reach these goals? When do I expect to achieve these goals?

Now, you are armed with a clear picture of your goals, and the reasons they are important to you. This should provide added level motivation to continue moving toward your goals.

Let's take the next step – Start an "Emergency Fund"

- Start small, but gradually increase the amount you are saving.
- Treat your savings plan as though it is an important bill, because it is!
- No excuses! Keep this account separate from your checking, or other savings accounts.

After your emergency fund reach one to two times your monthly income, start putting some of your money into certificates of deposit (CD) until you have at least the equivalent of six times that amount in your emergency fund.

You will be able to earn a higher return in a CD than in a savings account, but still have money available for true emergencies. It may be a good idea to lock your CD's in for at least one year. I suggest that you should ladder your CD's. In other words, if you have two or more CD's, each CD will mature in a different month. I suggest that they be spaced at least three to six months apart. For example, if each CD is $500, you would have a CD that would mature in different months. In this manner, you would have money available for emergencies, but would be earning a higher rate of return than in a regular savings account.

Your emergency fund should be large enough to cover your automobile and home insurance deductibles. Once your emergency fund is large enough to cover the previously mentioned items above, and other periodic bills, you may elect to self- insure future dental costs.

Identify your current monthly income and expenses

To develop a budget that is appropriate for your lifestyle, you'll need to identify your current monthly income and expenses. You can write the information down with a pencil and paper, or you can use one of the many software programs available that are designed specifically for this purpose.

Start by adding up all of your income. Next, add up all of your expenses. You'll also want to make sure that you have identified any periodic expenses, such as holiday gifts, car maintenance, home repair, and so on. To make sure that you're not forgetting anything, it may help to look through canceled checks, credit card bills, and other receipts from the past year. Finally, as you list your expenses, it is important to remember your financial goals. **Treat your goals as expenses, and purpose to contribute toward them regularly.**

Evaluate your budget

Once you've added up all of your income and expenses, and have compared the difference, then you will know if your budget is negative, positive, or break-even. If you find yourself at break-even, you'll need to make some adjustments, until you have a positive cash flow. Look at your expenses closely, and cut down on your discretionary spending. Don't worry! It will take determination, time, self-discipline, and you'll eventually get it right. If, your total income is breakeven, or less than your expenses, you should read chapter six to find more ways to get more mileage out of your budget.

Examples of prioritizing your expenses for payment:

1. Mortgage or rent.
2. Pay all loans that are secured by collateral. Normally, these should be given first priority of payment.
3. Transportation to work. You can't earn money if you don't have a way to work.
4. Health insurance
5. Food. You can ask for help with food from friends, church, charities, or government agencies.

Give your budget regular attention.

You'll need to monitor your budget periodically and make changes when necessary. But keep in mind that you don't have to keep track of every penny that you spend. Close estimates are fine. I suggest that you round up your figures in situations where it is feasible. In fact, the less record keeping you have to do, the easier it will be to stick to your budget. Above all, be flexible, and have fun. **Any budget that is not flexible is likely to fail.** So be prepared for the unexpected (e.g., leaky roof, flat tires, plumbing leaks, leak, lawn mower repairs).

Tips to help you stay focused on your budget goals

- Involve the entire family in helping to come up with ways to get more steam from your budget: Agree on a budget up front. Always meet regularly to evaluate your progress. Offer small rewards to whoever comes up with an idea that can be used.
- Stick to the basics: Save more, reduce your expenses to a minimum. Continue to search for opportunities that will enhance your budget. Make a plan, and be prepared to stick to it. But don't allow your plan to be so inflexible, that it will hamper your search to educate yourself about other opportunities that may be available.
- Stay disciplined: You should make an effort to make "budgeting" a part of your daily routine, without making it a pain in the neck. Brain-storm for creative ways to make it fun and rewarding.

- Start your new budget at a time when it's will be easiest to follow and stick with. (e.g., the beginning of the year, as opposed to right before the holidays).
- Find a budgeting system that fits your needs. Check with your local discount or office supply store for inexpensive software. Instead, you may choose to use the "envelope system" we discussed earlier to track your expenses. It works like this: First, write the name of each bill on a separate envelope. Next write the date each bill is due, the amount due, or other important information on each envelope. Place your payment in each envelope. Also, label one envelope "Income".
- Distinguish between expenses that are "wants" (e.g., video games) and expenses that are "needs" (e.g., food). Example: Stay clear of pre-prepared items as much as possible, because of higher purchase costs.
- Build small, regular rewards into your budget, especially when you accomplish one of your goals. (e.g., eat out every other week, ice cream, movie, family cookout, etc.)
- You must avoid using credit cards to pay for everyday expenses: It may seem like you're spending less, but your credit card debt will continue to increase if you continue to add new debt. Only carry your credit cards when you are traveling out of town.

Periodic Expenses- Periodic expenses are expenses that don't have to be paid every month, such as property taxes or automobile tags. It is still important to know what these expenses are, and how much you need to save in order to pay them in full when the bill due.

Things you want to save and invest for:

(Examples are home, auto, education, emergencies, vacation or cruise). Make a list in order of importance from top to bottom. *Divide the cost of your goal by the number of years in which to accomplish each goal. This is the amount that needs to be included in your saving plan each month. Adjust the year you wish to make your purchase until you have a savings amount that is realistic for you.*

You want to save for?	Cost	Year	How much to save each month
Total amount you need to save (things your want to save for).	$		

Transfer this total to the expense part of your budget sheet in chapter one, because you should be saving this amount each month.

Your quarterly bills are: **Amount due**

Estimate upward or rounding-upward is suggested. It is better to overestimate than to underestimate

Bill Description	Amount Due $
Total quarterly bills are	$

Divide the total due by 4 to know what you need to save each month. Place this amount in your monthly expense sheet as a monthly expense. You must include this amount in your savings in your budget.

Your semi-annual bills are: **Amount due**

Total semi-annual bills are	$

Divide the total amounts by six (6) to find out what you must save monthly. You must include your total amount in your monthly savings plan in your budget.

Your annual bills are: **Amount due**

Total annual bills are	$

Divide this amount by 12 so you will know how much to save monthly. Post as a monthly expense in your budget. This amount should be included in your saving plan in your budget.

Bills that you owe, but you are not making payments on:

Description	Payment Amount	Balance	Rate of interest
Total bills you owe, but are not making payments on: $			

Note: Do not show these debts in the income and expense part of your budget until you begin making payments.

Your Monthly Income

LIST ALL OF YOUR BILLS. (MONTHLY INCOME & EXPENSE BUDGET)

This is the month of: _____

Budget tips:

1. *Keep it flexible. Don't drive everyone nuts. Remember to keep it fun.*
2. *If you are married, review it together with your mate often.*
3. *Treat savings as though it is a bill.*
4. *You may use the envelope system if you don't have budgeting software.*

Income	
Your take home pay $	
Dividends earned $	
Public Assistance $	
Other Income $	
Total Income $	

Income

Take Home Pay $_____   (after taxes & payroll deductions)

Take Home Pay $_____   (after taxes & payroll deductions)

Your Monthly Expenses

(List all monthly expenses) **If you don't have budgeting software please make 12 copies of this page and the next page (for each month of the year).** *The goal is to make sure you can cover the first priorities such as food, clothing, housing, health care, insurance, education, retirement, and savings.*

Housing & Utilities

Rent or mortgage	$
Internet	$
Water	$
Electric/Heating/Cooling	$
Other	$
Other	$
Total Housing & Utilities	$

Transportation

Auto license tags	$
Automotive Insurance	$
Fuel	$
Driver's license	$
Other	$

Food

Eating out	$
School lunches	$
Groceries	$
Other	$
Total Food	$

Miscellaneous

Childcare	$
Cable/Satellite TV	$
Other	$
DVD/CD rental or purchase	$
Other	$
Total Miscellaneous	$

Clothing

Underwear	$
Outerwear, personal	$
Work clothes	$
Other	
Total Clothing	$

Medical

Doctor bills	$
Dental bills	$
Other	$
Total Medical Bills	

Recreation & Entertainment

Vacation	$
Other	$
Total Recreation & Entertainment	$

Savings & Investing

401 K saving	$
Emergency fund	$
Other	$
Total Savings & Investing	$

Total of Periodic Bills

Quarterly bills	$
Semi-annual bills	$
Annual bills	$
Other bills	$
Total Periodic Bills	$

Charity

Tithes	$
Offerings	$
Other charities	$
Total Charities	$

Education

College Savings	$
Other	$
Total Education	$

Taxes

Property Taxes	$
Income Taxes	$
Auto License Tags	$
Other Taxes	$
Total Taxes	$

Other debts

Credit Cards	$
Other Debts	$
Total Other Debts	$

Total Expenses .... $_____

Cash Flow Analysis: This amount can be negative (-) or positive (+). If your amount is negative, you must keep searching for ways to reduce expenses or increase your income until you have a positive amount. Break even is when your income and expenses are the same, however this is rare. A surplus (positive cash flow) is when your income exceeds your expenses.

Record your total income here $_____. Record your total expenses here $_____.
Subtract your total expenses from your total income. Record the difference here $_____.
If you have a negative difference, place a (-) symbol beside it.

If your have a negative difference, you should read chapter six. You will find suggestions that can help lower expenses until you have a positive cash flow.

General Budget Guidelines

This chart shows some flexible guidelines on how much of your income should go toward different expenses. Each category will vary. You will need to make adjustments to suit your particular personal ambitions, family goals, and other situations.

20-25%	Housing
10-18%	Transportation/Automotive
7-16%	Food & Household items
5-8%	Miscellaneous
3-5%	Clothing
3-10%	Medical/Dental
5-8%	Recreation
5-10%	Utilities
10-16%	Savings & Investing
5-18%	Other Debts

NET WORTH BALANCE SHEET

Assets (List all the things that you own)

Savings Account	$
Checking Account	$
Savings Account	$
Certificates of Deposits	$
Individual Retirement Account	$
Life Insurance (Cash Surrender Value)	$
Other Assets	$
Home (Market Value)	$

Profit Sharing (Equity)	$
Clothing & Jewelry (Quick sale value)	$
Other Real Estate	$
Stock (Market Value)	$
Mutual Funds (Market Value)	$
Other Investments	$
Keogh Plans	$
Furniture and Appliances	$

Money Owed to you	$
Other	$
Other	$
Total Assets You Own	$

* Please don't forget to include debts that you owe, but you are not currently making payments on.

List all your debts (Liabilities) Include things that you are co-signed for.

Description of debt	Payment	Interest Rate	Balance
Credit Card#1			
Credit Card#2			
Credit Card#3			
Credit Card#4			
Credit Card#5			
Loan#1			
Loans you are co-signed for			
Student Loans			
2nd Mortgage			
Home Equity loan			
Personal Debts: (Family, friends, etc.)			
Total Liabilities	$		

Net worth Balance Sheet Assessment

What is my net worth? It is thee difference between what you owe and what you owe. This difference can be negative or positive.

How much do you own? (assets)	$
How much do you owe? (liabilities)	$
Your Net Worth is (subtract liabilities from assets	$

Show a negative amount with this negative symbol (-). An ideal goal to work toward is to have liabilities equal 5% or lower than your total assets.

Your Business Sales and Expenses, Assets and Liabilities

Sales	$
Expenses (subtract expenses from sales)	$
Difference (+) (-)	$

Assets (the amounts the business owns)

Cash on hand	$
Real Estate	$
Equipment	$
Stock, Bonds	$
Equipment	$
Supplies	$
Other	$
Total Business Assets	$

Liabilities (amounts that the business owes)

Taxes Due	$
Notes Due	$
Other	$
Total liabilities	$

Total Business Assets	$
Total Business Liabilities	$
(subtract liabilities from assets)	
Total Difference	$

CHAPTER TWO
ELEVATE YOUR MINDSET & PERSONALITY

Chapter Two Objectives: We seek to challenge your current way of thinking and handling situations, so you can create positive outcomes more consistently. We promote the idea that a positive mental mindset reduces emotional harm, and increases your efficiency in all areas of your life, to include financial issues.

List the most important sixteen things you are grateful and thankful for:

Things that will hinder a creative mindset and personality

- Majoring in minor things.(Distractions)
- Fear of stepping outside of your comfort zone.
- Failure to recognize and take reasonable risks.
- Self-serving tunnel vision.
- A resistance to help so others can succeed.
- Resistance to necessary change.
- Poor spiritual relationships and problem solving skills.

Tips that can help you elevate your mindset and personality

1. Repent for your past misdeeds. There is no better way to prepare for the rest of your life than to wipe the slate clean and start again. No matter what happens from this point, you can face it better. Get a clear image of what you want to do with the remainder of your life, but be flexible enough to have a plan A, B, or even C, and beyond, if necessary. Always pray and ask God for guidance in your choices.
2. Stop being pre-judgmental of others. Learn to think and see the positive in every situation. It is imperative that you gather enough information about a situation or people before forming an opinion.
3. Picture yourself having obtained the expected end of your goals. Be sure to write them down. What are your goals? What benefits do you expect when you reach your goals?
4. Examine your behavior. They really reflect what you believe. Replace your bad behaviors and habits with good ones.

5. Make up your mind to be responsible for your actions, even when you make a mistake.
6. Rethink your values. Make sure they are in line with biblical principles. Renewing your mind to a new way of thinking is a must, if you expect to reach your goals and the purpose in your life.
7. Make sure you know what your skills are. Identify the ones you are weak in, and the areas in which you are strong. Your skills and talents represent your capacity to serve God through your fellowman, and how you will earn a living in life. To the extent that you use them, will help determine where you can live, work, and play.
8. Be thankful each day that you are alive, celebrate often, and reward yourself, and others, even in small ways that matter.
9. Think like a victor, not a victim. Don't seek revenge. That is reserved for God. Don't waste precious time trying to get even, instead continue to do unto others as you would have them do unto you.
10. You must practice becoming a more effective listener.
11. You should pray and meditate daily with the understanding that it is not always how long you pray, but the sincerity of your relationship with God.
12. Be sure to do physical exercise regularly. Example: My minimum goal is to exercise at least two times a week.
13. Learn to recognize valid opportunities at home, work, and recreation times.
14. **Make it a point to be teachable.** Often-times many people sabotage their personal growth by not listening to what others have to say. Make it a habit of being around people you can learn from, and perhaps support you in times of need.
15. Don't be so quick to make sure you get credit for your good deeds or ideas.
16. Stop complaining and justifying negative situations. Keep in mind that if you see something that needs to be improved for the better, don't pass the buck, it's up to you.
17. Become principal minded: Practice honesty, hard work, and diligence, etc.
18. Seek inter-dependency, not co-dependency.
19. Think and act out of the box to get greater than normal results.
20. Turn your cell phone off for at least one hour each day. Spend some time with yourself.
21. When someone does something good, give credit where credit is due.

Below please write a poem about yourself, such as the one below. Make up your own words that reflect the positive things about yourself. Use your name often.

Example: I AM BETTIE

I am made in the image of God. I am Bettie
I am kind and friendly.
I am loving, and forgiving. I am Bettie
I have small brown lips
I am happiest when I make others happy. I am Bettie.
A big bright smile
Short, but bright like the morning star. I am Bettie.

It is entitled: I AM -------------------- (Insert your name)

If you need additional space feel free to use an extra sheet of paper.

True /False   Personality Quiz -How do you see yourself?

1. _____ I enjoy helping people that are less fortunate than me.
2. _____ **I forgive people when they do bad things to me.**
3. _____ I celebrate the success of others.
4. _____ I exercise or walk at least two times each week.
5. _____ I am eager to learn new things.
6. _____ I will make proactive efforts to be a friendly person.
7. _____ I am sincerely sorry for the wrong things I have done.
8. _____ I sometimes do things I am afraid or uncomfortable to do.
9. _____ I appreciate the small things that people do for me.
10. _____ I have a positive attitude most of the time.
11. _____ I get plenty of rest most of the time.
12. _____ I don't normally take on too many tasks at one time.
13. _____ I am a generous person.
14. _____ I don't make excuses when I can't get something done.
15. _____ **I am a priceless person.**
16. _____ I will spend time trying to get even when someone does me wrong.
17. _____ I reach out to others who have a real need with compassion.
18. _____ I will make efforts to solve problems, not look for a quick fix.
19. _____ I work smarter, not harder.
20. _____ I will be open to coaching and continued learning.
21. _____ I will make every effort to be an effective communicator.
22. _____ I am thankful for every day I am allowed to live.
23. _____ I try to encourage others when they have problems.
24. _____ It's important that I grow and improve in all areas of my life.
25. _____ I always try to give good service on my job.

26. _____ **It's not alright to lie to reach a goal, or get something I want.**
27. _____ I seek the approval of others, rather than do the right thing.
28. _____ I practice being a good listener.
29. _____ I don't blame God when things go wrong.
30. _____ I make efforts to stay informed about current events.
31. _____ I do physical exercise at least two times a week.
32. _____ I read books and seek ways to increase my general knowledge.
33. _____ I am not afraid to question and prove the things I believe.
34. _____ After I pay bills, I don't feel broke.
35. _____ I say, "thank you" when others do something nice for me.
36. _____ **I try to treat others in the way I would like to be treated.**
37. _____ I spend my income on the things I want, then on the things I need.
38. _____ I did not get road rage in the last 12 months.
39. _____ I pray for everyone, even my enemies.
40. _____ Each problem that I face represents an opportunity to improve.

Give yourself 1 point for each true response. Points earned. _____

CHAPTER THREE
SETTING YOUR SHORT, MID-TERM AND LONG TERM GOALS

The objectives of this lesson: In this chapter you will learn how to set, monitor and reach your goals. Here, you will list your short, mid-term, and long term objectives and goals. Additionally, you will be able to organize your plan of action by priorities, and to make modifications to your plan if evaluation data indicates they are needed.

A good written plan of actions should include at minimum the following elements.

1. Access the situation – This is the fact finding part. List the resources that you may need to reach your goals. An example would be: If you wanted to start a lawn service or become a beautician, you could list the classes, training, and equipment you may need to accomplish this goal. Also list a date you reasonably expect to accomplish each.

2. Elevate the way you think – Faith actions instead of actions out of fear. Always look for the good in every situation. Don't wait for perfection to get started.

3. Setting goals and objectives – By setting goals, you now have a way of clarifying your goals. You will also be able to measure your progress because you are clear about what direction you must proceed.

4. Implementing your written plan – This is your opportunity to organize your efforts and resources in the order you desire for them to happen.

5. Maximizing relationships and environment – Your connection with people and events that will support you rather than the ones that drain you mentally.

6. Minimizing your everyday expenses. **Learn to ask yourself, "Do I really have to buy this product or service"?** Consider starting a small business from home to help reduce your taxes. In future sessions we will be presenting ways in which to accomplish this with minimum effort.

7. Connecting to support systems - Help is available when you need it. Start attending functions where you may expect to meet people with similar interest as yours. **Make it a habit of reading at least one book at least every three months.**

8. Organize for growth and maturity - Organize your work. Prepare a daily schedule of the things you want to accomplish for tomorrow, the day or night before. Delegate tasks where possible to free up your time.

9. Creating cushions to reduce risks – Never take risks where the risks are far out-weigh the rewards. Therefore, if you don't have health or life insurance, you must make this a top priority in your budget.

10. Increasing and replace your income (residual) Very few wealthy people work by the hour. They earn most of their income by forming relationships with other people, allowing them to better leverage their time, energy, and resources.

11. Maximizing your credibility. Work on mending past relationships with others. **Examine your credit report at least once a year.**

12. Review each chapter of this book at least quarterly. Evaluate your strategies. Add as necessary. Delete or revise strategies that are not working.

The following are some things that you can do that will help you reach your goals:

- Share your goals with only a few select people.
- List your goals, review them to check your progress often (weekly)
- Organize your goals into three groups (short term, mid-term, long term)
- Prioritize each goal in each group in the order of importance
- Beside each, list several things you can do to help each goal come to pass. (Remember, don't break any spiritual laws in order to force your goals to happen: for example – do not steal- always be honest – never misuse people)
- Do something to reach your goals everyday, even if it is something small.
- Revise your goals to meet changing conditions.

Why most people don't achieve their goals:

1. They don't have a clear vision of what they really want.
2. No written goals to remind you what areas on which you need to be focusing.
3. They fail to think for themselves. It's alright to get advice, but any decision to act is still your responsibility. No written goals to remind you what areas on which you need to be focusing.

ELEMENTS OF A GOOD PLAN TO HELP YOU REACH YOUR GOALS

To be effective your goals should be:

1. Must be **purpose driven** - What are the reasons you want to accomplish your goals?
2. **Specific** -   Written on paper. You must have clearly defined goals. You must describe what you wish to accomplish with as much detail as possible.
3. **Measurable** -   Describes in terms that can be evaluated, such as when you expect a certain thing to happen. Identifies the conditions in which performance is expected.
4. **Challenging** -   It will take energy and discipline to accomplish your goals.
5. **Guiding Principles** -   It must stay with the boundaries set by spiritual and natural laws.
6. **Simple**- Step by step. Even the biggest things in life are made of smaller things. Sometimes, you can understand things better when you break them down into bite size steps.
7. **Flexible**- You should have a plan A, B, C and so on. You should also train yourself to earn a living using more than one skill. There will be times when you may add or delete some of your goals as your skills and other situations change.
8. **Duplicable**- Your process can be performed by others. A good example would be a recipe for a particular kind of cake or pie. In other words, if you can help enough people be successful, and get what they want out of life, you have a greater chance of getting what you want out of life.

9. **Faith driven**- In your heart you have to know that what you are trying to accomplish matters, and are worth your time and efforts.
10. **Minimizes risks**- Create cushions and safeguards against the impact of risks as you move toward your goals.
11. **Minimizes waste and excess**- To give you a greater chance of success, it is necessary to get the best use of your time, resources, energy, etc.
12. **Established priorities**- Depending on the moment, everything in life can be put into a ranking of importance.
13. **Must be balanced**. A good example of importance would be as follows: God, family, others, and yourself.
14. **Must be contingent**- Always have more than one way to accomplish your tasks, such as a plan A, B, or C.
15. **Desire/passion driven**- If what you are doing does not turn you on, then you are apt to quit when the going gets tough.
16. **Realistic** -A goal that you believe that you are capable of achieving. There must be achievable deadlines.
17. **Timely**-You must set an estimated date of completion for each goal, with the understanding that it will probably change.
18. **Beneficial**-There must be expected benefits for you and others.

Example of some goals you may want to set, work or plan toward

(You should feel free to use or revise any of these in your short, midterm, and long term goals)

1. If you are a two-income family you may want to work toward paying all bills from the income of the individual that has the highest income, and saving or investing the other paycheck.
2. **Place as many of your bills on auto pay as possible.**
3. Spend at least one hour a week sharpening your skills, or reading.
4. Set up a trust account to ease the burdens of the next generations of your offspring. **Never withdraw any of your principal, and never withdraw more than 85% of the earnings of your trust.** This strategy should promote perpetual growth.
5. If you must borrow, secure the loan yourself.
6. Limit yourself to having only one or two credit cards.
7. Maintain at least two weeks food supply at home for emergencies.
8. A debt load of less than 1% of your gross annual income.
9. To eventually save or invest more than 10% of your gross income.
10. **Save a portion of all income that you receive.**
11. Schedule family time at least one or more times a week.
12. Give generously to church and charity.
13. Save for things you want to buy, rather than make new debt.
14. Take at least four vacations per year.
15. Increase your level of education.
16. Save for your children's education.

Decide where you want to go in life, and how to start making plans to get there. Any plans that you make should consider the following things:

- You should always pray and ask God for guidance. How long you pray or mediate is not as important as being sincere. Then plan your strategy.
- Decide where you want to be in life. Define what success means to you.
- Be willing to share with others. Be willing to help others reach their goals.
- Don't be afraid to challenge your current beliefs and habits.
- List the problems and challenges you are facing. List as many possible solutions for each challenge or problem. After considering the consequences of each solution, pick the best one and implement it.
- List your strong points. List possible ways to improve each strong point.
- List your weak points. List possible ways to improve each of your weak points.

Why you should have written goals? Written objectives will give you a target to aim at or focus your attention toward. They give you a sense of direction and a glimpse of where you are going, and what benefits you can expect when they are achieved. They motivate you to act to get a reward and benefit. Objectives offer a way of measuring your level of success at any given point. **For each of your goals you should have an idea of: why, what, when, who, how, and where.** There will be many times that you will not know these answers. That is ok, because you will always have to use a measure of faith to accomplish any worthwhile goal.

Goals have to be envisioned, planned, organized, controlled, and evaluated. Your goals must be flexible to meet the changing condition of your environment. You must seek to balance your life, but remain focused on your goals.

I feel the following are my strengths:

- How I intend to use the skills I have now?

Put a check mark beside each item as you accomplish it. Also list it in your short, midterm, or long term goals.

- Additional skills I will need to reach my goals in life

_____
_____
_____
_____
_____
_____
_____
_____

Put a check mark beside each item as you accomplish it.

- These are ways I intend to contribute to society in a positive way now?

_____
_____
_____
_____
_____
_____
_____
_____
_____
_____

Put check mark beside each item as you accomplish it. Also place these in your short, midterm, and long term goals.

Name at least eight things you feel strong about and would like to accomplish before you die?

_____
_____
_____
_____
_____
_____
_____
_____
_____

Put a check mark beside each item when you accomplish it. Also place these in your short, midterm, and long term goals.

There are different kinds of goals. Please list a few below:

- Educational goals

_____
_____
_____
_____
_____
_____
_____
_____

Put a check mark beside each item as you accomplish it. Also place these in your short, midterm, and long term goals.

- Spiritual goals (List a date you expect each to happen)

Put a check mark beside each item as you accomplish it. Also place these in your short, midterm, and long term goals.

- Financial goals (List a date you expect each to happen)

Put a check mark beside each item as you accomplish it. Also place these in your short, midterm, and long term goals.

- Health & Medical goals (Examples: Yearly physical examination).

Put a check mark beside each item as you accomplish it. Also place these in your short, midterm, and long term goals.

- Debts (Eliminate or minimize debts). Example: Keep my total debts less than 1% of my gross annual income.

- Physical goals (List a date you expect each to happen):
  (Example: Lose 10 lbs weekly).

_____

_____

Survey Quiz	**Setting Goals**	**True / False**
A. _____	I have read chapter one.	
B. _____	I have read chapter two.	
C. _____	I have written my short term goals.	
D. _____	I have written my mid-term goals.	
E. _____	I have written my long term goals.	
F. _____	I have written my spiritual goals.	
G. _____	I have written my educational goals.	
H. _____	I have written my financial goals.	
I. _____	I have written my health goals.	
J. _____	I set goals that will benefit others also.	

Give yourself one point for each true response. Points earned. _____.

CHAPTER FOUR

IMPLEMENTING YOUR <u>WRITTEN</u> <u>PLAN OF ACTION</u>

Chapter Objectives: Our aim is to present systematic, step by step ways to organize, optimize your time, efforts, and resources to help reach goals you set.

Belief – The basis for action. I am convinced that people don't just do things for no reason, but are motivated to do things. **How we respond to situations, is a true reflection of what we believe.** When we believe great things, great things can happen. We were all fashioned by the Creator with the abilities to live our lives in abundance. All have the potential for achievement and fulfillment. **For the most part, your failure or success in life will be shaped by what you choose to believe and practice.**

If you can believe, you have a greater opportunity for achievement. Your actions reflect what you really believe, and your level of faith. When faith comes, it brings the commitment that can bring about change. People of little faith, are easily swayed by the presentation of false evidence of the present, rather than possibilities of the future. What we choose to place our faith in will set the limits to which we can aspire. To have faith in ineffective principles will cause you to behave in non-productive and destructive ways. So be careful what you believe or speak. Now! Let's take another step toward your journey to: GO UP IN A DOWN ECONOMY.

Your Implementation checklist should be simple and systematic. It should allow you to systematically pay down, or eliminate your debts, and obtain a safer, higher income- to- expense cash flow.

Start implementing your plan to get out of debt, or stop living paycheck to paycheck.

Place a check mark beside each item as you complete it.

1. **Assessment of your situation. (Chapter One)**

   - _____ List facts surrounding your situation: personal, financial, spiritual, etc.
   - _____ Read or review Chapter One.

2. **Order your credit reports. (Chapter One)**

   - _____ Get a copy of your credit reports (3) and compare account balances. You are eligible to receive free credit reports from each agency annually. You are also eligible to receive free credit reports when you are denied credit. Also, make efforts to correct any errors found on your credit reports when they arrive.

3. **Calculate your total monthly income (Chapter One)**

   - _____ Include income from all sources.

4. **Calculate your money expenses (Chapter One)**

- _____   Estimate them until you know the exact amounts.

5. **Calculate your total debt. (Chapter One)**

- _____   Include loans that you have cosigned.
- _____   Include the latest statements from creditors.

6. **Getting into the black (positive cash flow) (Chapter One & Chapter Six)**

- _____   Total your monthly income.
- _____   Subtract your monthly expenses.
- _____   Calculate a negative or positive difference.
- _____   *Proceed to the next step if you have a positive cash flow. If you still have a negative cash flow, see chapter 6 for tips on lowering your expenses.*

7. **List all your assets (Chapter One)**

- _____   List all you own or control.

8. **List all of you liabilities (Chapter One)**

- _____   List all you owe (personal and commercial)

9. **Determine if your net-worth is negative or positive (Chapter One)**

- _____   List total assets
- _____   List total liabilities
- _____   Calculate a negative or positive difference

If your net worth is positive please continue. If your net worth is negative, see chapter six.

10. **Create a current personal profile of yourself (Chapter One)**

- _____   You must be honest about your answers and your situation.

11. **Prioritize all of your debts to determine the order to pay down your creditors. (Chapter One)**

- _____   Negotiate lower interest rates where possible.
- _____   1st priority, secured loans such as home, auto, 1st and 2nd mortgages.
- _____   Pay the minimum amount on accounts that do not charge interest.
- _____   <u>Make a list of the 5 smallest credit accounts</u> that you pay interest.

Creditor Description	Date Due	Interest Rate

Note: Even though your minimum payment due will decrease, continue to pay according to your plan. Keep up this pattern as you pay all your bills.

There are the two basic methods for paying off your credit cards. Below are a few tips to help you decide which to use.

1. **Highest interest rate first.** Paying off the credit card with highest interest rate first will normally allow you to pay less interest in the long run. When the highest interest rate card also has the highest balance, it will take the longest to pay off. The down-side of this method is: It's easy to lose motivation paying off your debt when it takes too long. That's one of the reasons why the "lowest balance first" method might be a better choice.

2. **Lowest balance first.** There are immediate tangible benefits to paying off the credit card with the lowest balance first. The lowest balances are easier and quicker to pay off. The extra money will allow you an opportunity to start building a cushion to cover financial shortfalls sooner. As you pay off a bill, you will have a feeling of accomplishment as motivation to keep you going. You can now start applying the extra money to other debts. **If you do not have a positive cash flow, this may be the best method to start using.** Once you have a positive cash flow, then you may want to switch to "paying the highest interest rate".

Pick the method that suites your situation best. Now that you have identified the method you are going to use to pay off your credit cards, let's get started! Next, write your debts down in the order you're going to pay them - either from highest interest rate to lowest interest rate or from lowest balance to highest balance. Write down the interest rate, balance, minimum payment, and date due. Then, direct as much as possible of your entire net income to paying off the credit card on the top of your list. You should send the minimum payment due, plus $1.00 or more, to all your other credit cards.

Once you've repaid the first credit card, line through it on your list. Now focus on the next card on the list. As before, pay a much as your income as you can toward this card. Keep repeating this process until all the cards have been paid off.

12. **Change the way your think, learn, and respond to life's situations.**

- _____ You should always look for the good in every bad situation.
- _____ Read or Review Chapter Two.

13. Recording and organizing your goals on paper.

- _____ Read or Review Chapter Three.

14. Implement your step by step written plan.

- _____ Read or Review Chapter Four.
- _____ Use your "Master Things To Do" List.
- _____ Use your short, midterm, and long term goals.

15. Building relationships that support you and your goals.

- _____ Read or Review Chapter Five

16. Reducing your day to day living (operating expenses).

- _____ Implement policies to reduce non essential costs and excessive waste.
- _____ Read or review Chapter Six.

17. Connect to support systems (environment).

- _____ Read or review Chapter Seven.

18. Systematic growth and maturity of your wealth.

- _____ Read or review Chapter Eight

19. Creating cushions to reduce the effects of risks and liabilities.

- _____ Start building your saving and investment plan.
- _____ Read or review Chapter Nine.

20. Income replacement and the creation of wealth.

- _____ Read or review Chapter Ten.

21. Maximizing your reputation and credibility.

- _____ Read or review Chapter Eleven.

22. Review your step by step plan often.

- _____ Add things to customize your plan to fit your specific goals.
- _____ Use your "Master Things to Do List".
- _____ Use your short, midterm, and long term goals list.
- _____ Make a list of failed strategies and why you think they didn't work.
- _____ Delete and replace strategies that are not working.
- _____ Write down things you wish to discuss at your next family financial meeting.

- _____ Write a brief note if you wish to share any success story or comment with our office.
- _____ Review each chapter at least every three to six months.
- _____ Review Chapter Twelve.

Survey Quiz   Implementing your plan of action

True / False

_____ I have made a conscious choice to minimize, or eliminate my debts.

_____ I am tracking my Income & Expenses.

_____ **I have a positive cash flow.**

_____ I will continue to think about ways to restrict my access to new debt.

_____ I will continue to look for ways to keep a positive cash flow.

_____ I will make every effort to be honest.

_____ I have listed all my income and expenses.

_____ I have listed all my assets.

_____ I have listed my bills smallest to largest.

_____ I added money to my emergency fund this pay period, or I already have one month savings in my emergency fund.

_____ I did not make any new debts in the last 60 days.

_____ I did not make any new debts in the last 120 days.

_____ **I have identified my secured debts.**

_____ I have not acquired any new debt in the last 12 months.

_____ I have not acquired new debt in the last 24 months.

_____ I have identified my non-secured credit accounts.

_____ **I am buying a home, I expect to have it paid off before I retire.**

_____ Establish a payment plan you are comfortable with. Contact each creditor in writing. Don't make promises that you can't keep.

_____ I reach out to people that are less fortunate than I.

_____ I have started saving, even if it is a small amount.

_____ I know how much I owe on each account.

_____ I know the value of the things I own.

_____ I know how much I earn monthly.

_____ I know how much I spend monthly.

_____ I did not pay any fees for maintaining my checking account in the last 6 months.

_____ I added money to my savings account in the last 30 days.

_____ I will reward myself and family in a small way each time we accomplish a goal.

Give yourself one point for each true response. Points earned. _____.

Please share with us!

We would like to share any successes that you experience with us. Briefly explain how this book may have helped you. You do not have to include your name. We hope this session benefited you. Remember, we welcome your suggestions and comments. Please make several copies of this page, so that from time to time, you can share with us and others that need to be encouraged.

Please mail all correspondence to:

Lawrence Surles Sr.
1545 Bingham Drive, Fayetteville, NC 28304-5525
Lawrence.surles@yahoo.com

My Goal is! - Picture This!

Make 25 copies of this checklist. Please list only one goal per sheet. It may not be necessary to use this method to reach simple goals. This sheet is optional, but you should feel free to use it for any midterm or long term goal.

My goal is:_____

Date I would like to accomplish this goal (Month / Day / Year) _____

Things I can do to help me accomplish this goal.

Draw a line through or place a check mark beside each item as you complete it.

I have satisfactorily completed this goal. Date (Month/Year) _____

CHAPTER FIVE
MAXIMIZING YOUR RELATIONSHIPS

Chapter Objectives: You will be introduced to various ways that will help you learn how to seek out, attract and maintain positive, supportive relationships you will need to help you grow and mature.

If you expect to become successful in any area of your life, you must seek out and establish successful relationships. If you expect to reach your goals in life, you must learn to establish new, fix old ones, strengthen, and discontinue some relationships.

Make every attempt to hang around people that can and will support you. You can't expect people to support your idea if you are not willing to share some of your expected successes with them. You can't make things happen in a vacuum. It has been said that the average person works for the positive changes they want, but the wealthy seeks to form relationships that will promote the positive changes they desire. It is essential that you form relationships that support your values. Good relationships will empower you with the information to act on your dreams, therefore giving you the opportunity to draw on the experience of others.

Every relationship you have is not meant to last a lifetime. In order to get on with your dream it may become necessary to discontinue or tone down some relationships that drain you. It does not mean you don't love them, but in order to make progress you may have to spend less time with them. It might be a good idea to attend social functions where you can meet others that are interested in similar things. Hang with Eagles, you're learn to think and soar like an Eagle. Truly successful people will be interested in you becoming successful also.

There are many ways to build positive relationships.

Relationships are built on trust. Your perceived character and competence are a vital part of building trust. When you extend trust to someone, you give them the opportunity to present themselves trustworthy. **Real trust is never instant, or by force, but is built over a period of time and experiences.** People tend to give more trust to people they perceive to have the best character, and level of competence. Relationships with the most transparency tend to have a higher level of trust.

Consider some of the following tips:

1. When you are having a conversation with others, focus the conversation on the other person. Be sure to ask questions. Resist the temptation of allowing yourself to be the focus of the conversation.
2. Set others up for success. Be willing to provide any useful information you may know, without basing it on "getting something in return".
3. Remember, everyone is different, but if you look hard enough, common interest can be found.

4. Become a cheerleader for others. Give credit where credit is due, and share in the accomplishments of others. Resist trying to steal the moment by mentioning something that you have accomplished.

5. Seek supporting relationships that build, instead of self-centered ones that leave you holding the bag.

6. Learn to conduct yourself in a way that clearly shows that you can be trusted. Find one or two people that you can confide in. Everyone should have someone to whom they are accountable to. When you are dealing with confidential issues, you need someone that you can trust enough to offer advice, or just to listen to you.

7. **Don't just say that you care about people, demonstrate love and concern.** There are times when you can take the time to send a thank you note, birthday card, and so on. Sometimes a phone call will go a long way in giving strength to a relationship.

8. Treat everyone as a VIP, with urgency and importance.

9. Be sure to make efforts that will strengthen your family relationship at home.

10. **A strong spiritual relationship with God will go a long way in helping you foster successful relationships with other people.**

11. Seek to build a year round relationship with your tax preparer. Ask them about things you can do during the year to reduce your income tax bill. You will be surprised how willing they are to help you. As a good gesture; send them a thank you card or a small gift afterward.

12. **If you expect respect from others, show mutual respect at all times.** This should hold true whether they are friend, enemy, rich, poor, or employee.

13. Frequent events where it is likely you will meet people that have similar interest as yours.

14. When conflicts arise, express your feeling, rather than attribute bad motives to others.

Survey Quiz   Maximizing your relationships

_____ I am reliable.
_____ I am intelligent.
_____ I am creative.
_____ I am a team player.
_____ I demonstrate love by my actions.
_____ Whenever a person tells me a secret, I can keep it secret.
_____ I am not judgmental of others.
_____ I give generous at church, or other charities.
_____ I make extra effort to schedule time with my family.
_____ I value the opinions of others.

CHAPTER SIX

FINDING WAYS TO MINIMIZE YOUR DAY TO DAY OPERATING EXPENSES AND REDUCE DEBTS

Chapter six objectives: Learn how to pay less for the basics, such as food, clothing, and shelter, so you can have more of things that you would desire to have. In addition, we will help identify areas of excess, waste, and inefficiency. You will learn new ways to cut your monthly expenses, so you can stabilize your budget, and have extra money to pay current bills, catch up on past due bills, and even start eliminating any debt you may have.

In order for you to minimize your day to day bills and expenses you can consider some of the following:

Look at every expenditure, no matter how small or large. Look for ways in which to lower each. Make sure your secured debts get first priority. Next, prioritize the remainder of your bills accordingly, starting with the highest interest rate debts first. If you have a negative cash flow, as an alternative, you might consider paying off your smallest debts first. If your high interest debts also have high balances, you could end up paying on an account for years before the entire balance has been repaid. Since smaller debts can be repaid quicker, many people opt to pay them first. This way you should experience victories soon. This will serve to encourage you to keep moving forward with your plan.

You should choose the method that will keep you encouraged to pay off your debts.

If getting the best value for your payments is most important, then the high-interest method is best. On the other hand, if you might become unmotivated by paying on a large debt for a long period of time, then starting with the smallest debt method will be better for you. Once you know how much you will be spending to pay off your debt, you can complete your plan. Put all of your debt-spending money towards your highest priority debt.

This will either be your smallest debt or the debt with the highest interest rate, depending on the method you choose. Pay this amount plus the minimum payment every month until the debt has been completely repaid. You must continue making the minimum payments on your other debts. Once you've paid off the first debt, combine the minimum payment from that debt with the extra amount you've allocated for repaying your debts and put it towards the debt with the next highest interest rate (or next smallest balance). Repeat this process until your debts have been completely repaid.

Ways to get out of the red (Stabilizing your budget so you can have a positive cash flow)

- Request a financial hardship plan that lowers the interest rate and minimum payment amount for six months to a year. Most companies offer one, so don't be bashful about asking.

- Be creative. Keep looking for ways to increase your income, reduce your expenses and risks. You must do whatever it takes to finally have a positive cash flow.
- Watch and question the small expenses. Stick to the basics. Go over each expense line by line. Don't be afraid to question any and all expenses. Leave no stone unturned. You will soon find that your take-home pay will begin to go a lot further.
- List your five (5) smallest bills, along with the interest rate you are being charged. Pay as much as possible on the one with the highest interest rate, while paying the minimum on the other four (4). See our example in chapter four.
- Have a yard sale, if you have things you don't want, or can't use anymore.
- Purchase used items instead of new ones.
- **Find less expensive ways to entertain yourself, family, or friends.**
- Consider the pros and cons of a consolidation loan. We will present a few basic considerations later in this chapter. Be sure to consult an Attorney, tax advisor, loan officer, or other competent parties.
- Find each bill that you pay. In Chapter Six, you will find a sample form that you can use. Write the name of the bill at the top of the page. Then number each line from 1 to 20, more if you need to. We have one in this book that you can make copies of. List as many ways you can think of to reduce that particular bill or expense. **It is very important to have a positive cash flow budget before you proceed to the next chapter.**

Ways to slow your impulse spending that steals the money you need to cover your essentials, such as food, shelter, and debt repayment

- Leave your credit cards at home when you are near home.
- One at a time, cut up, but don't cancel your credit cards, as this can lower your credit rating. You can get a new card issued, if you choose, when balances are at zero.
- Buy at discount stores instead of convenient stores. Always make a listing before shopping.
- Example: **Wait at least 24 hours before you spend more than $50 on any one item.**
- Set a budget and stick to it.

These are examples of prioritizing your spending based on importance.

- Shelter
- Secured debts
- Food and water
- Unsecured debts
- Clothing
- Debts on which you are not being charged interest.
- Other _____.

Tips to minimize your tax obligations:

- Delay your taxes as long as possible without incurring penalties.

- Take all the deductions and credits that you are allowed by law.
- Make efforts to invest in non-taxable investments such as municipal bonds
- Inquire at your place of employment about pre-tax deductions.
- Maximize your IRA and 401K contributions.
- If you are self employed contribute to an SEP or Keogh plan.
- Start a <u>simple </u>home based business for income and tax advantages. See chapter 10.

Assessment to determine if a debt consolidation loan may be right for you:

The goal of loan consolidation should be to consolidate two or more balances with higher interest rates into one easier to handle, less costly loan. Keep in mind that you are not eliminating your debts, but only shifting them. If your budget allows it, you should keep paying as close to the original payment totals of your old loans as possible. Listed below, are a few tips that can help you determine whether borrowing against your home's equity is a wise move.

- If you will be able to get a fixed interest rate that is lower than the rate you are now paying on your current debts.
- If you are in a shaky job market.
- If you are having serious problems in your marriage, or having thoughts of divorcing.
- A debt repayment plan, to include a firm decision to not take on any new debt. More than 70% of people in the USA who take out a home equity loan, or other types of loans to pay off credit card debt end up with the same debt load or higher in less than three years.
- If a lower payment will give you a positive cash flow of 15% or more of your take- home pay.
- Make sure you are actually saving money before signing new loan papers. Make sure you understand the total interest you will be paying on your loan. Calculate interest and fees on all your existing accounts to determine the total of the payments you now make. Then compare those amounts with the consolidation loan numbers to make sure it truly is a better choice.
- If you don't own a home, or something to secure the debt, you probably will not get the lowest interest rate.

To determine if re-financing your home is right for you, at minimum we suggest:

- If you have at least 10% equity in your home.
- You should be getting an interest rate at least 2 points lower on your new loan.
- Consult your tax advisor, or local realtors for professional advice. It is always wise to get a second or third opinion.

If you decide to refinance you should consider, at minimum the following suggestions:

- You should have at least a 720 credit score or above in order to be eligible to receive the best interest rates.
- Be sure to shop several lenders for the best offer. Don't accept an offer until you have shopped around.

- Be sure that you lock in a fixed interest rate. Stay away from variable rate loans.
- Never sign documents you don't understand or have not read completely.
- Borrowing too much, such as borrowing more than the market value of your property.
- **Be sure to obtain written estimation of your closing costs.**
- Be willing to walk away from a deal you are uncomfortable with.
- Be careful about refinancing too often.
- Ask questions about pre-payment penalties.
- Consult your tax advisor or several local realtors. It is always wise to get a second or third opinion.

At a minimum, consider debt consolidation using your credit card if:

- You can get an equivalent or lower fixed rate for the life of the loan.
- You commit to paying more than the minimum monthly payment.
- **You will tear up your credit cards you transferred the balances from, so you won't have the opportunity to run their balances up again.**

Tips for paying down debt and reducing expenses and debts:

Transportation

1. **Estimate the amount you need** to save each month for periodic expenses such as auto insurance & tags, annual automotive inspections, etc. Add this estimated amount to the amount you are currently saving.

2. **Turn your home into an additional tax advantage.** Having a home based business does not have to be a pain in the neck. Some are very simple. Even if you have a business elsewhere, it is a good idea to maintain an office in your home as a tax advantage. We have investigated hundreds of business opportunities. In this book, we will share one we believe to be compatible with any of your career and personal goals. It is designed so it will not interfere with your current job, and still obtain great results without the traditional hassle associated with owning most businesses. See Chapter 10.

3. **Check your vehicle's tire pressure at least monthly.** Things like under-inflated tires and dirty air filters can reduce your gas mileage up to 3%. Pick up an inexpensive tire gauge at the auto parts store, and check the pressure every month. You can also purchase an inexpensive tire inflator at your local auto parts or discount store.

4. **Carpool a few times a week.** Take turns carpooling with a friend or coworker, especially if they live close to you. Pick them up and take them home this week, and next week allow them to return the favor. You will save wear and tear on both vehicles. This should also considerably extend the life of your present vehicle. Chances are you will foster a better relationship with each other during your ride to work.

5. **Raise your insurance deductibles.** Assuming you have a proper emergency fund in place, raise deductibles on insurance policies. The difference in a $500 deductible and a $1,000 deductible on your car insurance policy can help reduce your monthly or semi-annual premiums. You should save or invest the difference of your lower payment. Maintain the amounts of your home and auto insurance deductible in your savings account or CD's.

6. **Consolidate errands into one trip.** Make a list of things you need to do. Consolidate all of your errands into one trip away from home, instead of driving back and forth several times a week from store to home.

7. **Ride a bike for short commutes.** I'm fortunate to live about 3 miles from my employer, so I regularly commute by scooter. If you happen to live close to stores, consider riding a bike or scooter for small errands. Take along a backpack, or put some panniers on your bike to carry things back home. A small scooter, 50 cc, can accomplish the same tasks – faster and less tiring.

8. **Unload the trunk, and remove unused cargo racks.** Added weight in the trunk reduces gas mileage.

9. **Wash your own car.** Make it a family project. Better yet, employ the kids and let them earn a little extra money instead of giving them an allowance.

10. **Buy a car after Christmas or the end of the year.** Most dealers are willing to offer deep discounts so they can reach their sales goals before the year ends. They are under more pressure to reach a deal then, which is usually good for the buyer.

11. **Pay at the pump.** When you need gas in your vehicle, pay at the pump, instead of going inside the store where you will be tempted by impulse items.

12. **Use cruise control on long trips.** There are studies that indicate your car may get about the same gas mileage with the air-conditioner on as opposed to letting the windows down creating drag from the wind.

13. **Avoid making rapid starts and stops with your vehicle.** Autos use more fuel in stop and go traffic. Fast starts and stops only add to the expense of operating your car.

14. **If you have cars that are insured, but will not be driving them for six months or more, consider canceling the insurance for a while to lower costs.** This can help you stabilize your finances in order to build a cushion for emergencies. Be sure to turn in your automobile license plates prior to canceling your insurance, to avoid any fines.

15. **If your job requires you to travel often,** consider the advantages of owning a GPS, to avoid mishaps, such as fewer missed appointments.

16. **When you make your last payment on your vehicle,** continue to put at least 50% to 100% of your vehicle payment into savings or investing. Therefore, if you decide to purchase another auto later, you should be able to pay for it in full, or very close to it.

17. **Once you have any emergency fund in place,** you may want to consider lowering your automotive insurance deductible. Then you will not have to nickel-and- dime your insurance carrier for small things. Too many small claims will normally cause you to be viewed as a high risk to the insurance carrier.

18. **Get your car serviced regularly** to make sure you get the best gas mileage.

19. **Consolidate errands.** Run all your errands in a single trip to avoid unnecessary driving. Consider having a "no drive day", unless you have an absolute emergency.

20. **Telecommute** if your employer will allow it. More companies are apt to consider such a move.

Home and Utilities

21. **Switch to cloth napkins.** Years ago, that's all they used at home. Cloth napkins are a great alternative to paper napkins, which increase waste and add to our non-food budget. It is still alright to have a couple rolls of paper napkins as a backup, for quests, and special occasions. Be sure to change them at least daily.

22. **If you must buy bottled water, buy bottled water at discount stores.** Once you drink the water, clean and refill the bottles with filtered tap water to use at home and work. Your friends will probably never know the difference.

23. **Drink tap water.** Buy a pitcher water filter from your local discount store. You can use it refill empty water bottles. Your friends won't know the difference, but your wallet will.

24. **Sign up for "Average billing" with your utility company.** This won't save you money, but it certainly helps the budgeting process by smoothing out seasonal ups and downs in your utility bills. You can usually do this after you have at least 12 months of service with the utility company (electric company). This will help take some of the surprises out of your electric bill.

25. **Switch to CFL lighting inside, and solar lighting outside.** CFL bulbs use much less energy than incandescent bulbs, and give off less heat. Solar lights used to line pathways

around your home run off a rechargeable battery that is charged up during the day by the sun, and lasts for several hours after dark.

26. **Cut the number of days your lawn is being watered**. An established lawn doesn't really need to be watered every day. In fact, daily watering can cause a shallow root system because grass roots don't have to work hard to find water. Water your lawn once or twice a week.

27. **Take a "quick" shower**. Get in, soap up, rinse off and get out. You will be surprised to see your water bills become lower.

28. **Consider water saving appliances**. Look for water saving appliances when purchasing new appliances.

29. **Run your ceiling fan** counter-clockwise in the summer months. Run the ceiling fan clockwise in the winter months to force warm air downward into occupied spaces.

30. **Consider refinancing your mortgage if you can get another at 2 or more percentage points lower**. Don't be too concerned about lowering your mortgage payment. Getting the lower rate is more important in the long run. Avoid "cash out" situations.

31. **Properly insulate your home**. This is especially important in the summer and winter months, when the extreme temperatures outside can affect your temperature inside and cause utility bills to be larger than normal. You may consider darker curtains in the summer to help block out sunlight. You will notice the several degrees difference in the temperature.

32. **Purchase and install a water heater blanket at your local hardware store**. This will help reduce the heat loss from your water heater (electric water heaters only).

33. **Purchase a good water restrictor for your shower**. This can save you perhaps 5-10% on your water bill. Many municipalities are beginning to require them, especially during hot dry summer months.

34. **Replace home air conditioner filter every month when in use**. Some manufacturers suggest changing your filter every 90 days, but systems may work better when changed once a month, especially in peak times like summer. Re-useable filters are also available, and can save a considerable amount of money over several years.

35. **Consider purchasing a programmable thermostat**. Studies show that saving can be substantial. You will be able to maintain a lower temperature when you are on a trip or away from home, and allow you to use less heat or air conditioning when you are not at home for extended periods of time.

36. **Consider awning.** Awning can reflect direct sunlight from your window, resulting in a slightly cooler temperature within your home. Besides, it would add to the appearance of your home.

37. **Unstop your commode.** The next time you have a stopped commode, try using your garden hose first, before calling a plumber.

38. **Trim hedges at home that offer burglars a place to hide,** or encourage them to enter your home while you are away. You can save the cost of replacing things that could have been stolen.

39. **Call your mortgage company.** There may be benefits to setting your mortgage up to be paid bi-monthly, instead of monthly.

40. **Slowly build your savings so you can pay an extra home payment** on your principal each year. Consult your mortgage company about any prepayment penalties prior to making any additional payments.

41. **Lower the setting on your hot water heater to its lowest setting,** normally around 115 degrees. Check with your local hardware store for a water heater jacket, if you have an electric water heater.

42. **Check with your local hardware store** for advice about thickness of insulation in your attic. Ask the electric or gas company, as whether they offer free or low cost energy audits.

43. **Consider canceling your home phone** and let your cell phone replace it for a while. You may be able to transfer (port) your home number to your cell phone.

44. **Examine your cellular phone plans.** Make sure you are not paying for national coverage if you only go out of your local coverage one or two times a year. Many companies offer a regional coverage, and will be happy to switch you to national if you begin to travel out of state often.

45. **Install a power strip.** Many appliances such as TV's, stereos and other home electronics use electricity while they are turned off. Some stores offer a surge protector that will turn off accessories when the main component is turned off.

46. **Buy a waste basket.** Stop buying trash bags. Check the size of the grocery bags used by the stores that you shop at. Buy a waste basket that would let your grocery bag serve as a trash liner.

47. **Don't pay someone for small repairs.** You would be surprised how much you can do on your own to avoid expensive repair charges around the house. Consider getting "Do it yourself repair" book from your local library.

48. **Check the insulation around your doors and windows** and replace when they have excessive wear. Windows are one of the biggest contributors to home heat loss. If you don't have double-insulated windows, you may want to put a clear plastic cover on the inside of your windows in the winter.

49. **If you have a dishwasher, use only the wash and rise cycle.** Skip the dry cycle, and let your dishes air dry. It saves wear and tear on your appliances and energy cost savings.

50. **A simple way to save.** Turn lights off when they are not in use.

51. **Keep drapes and window curtains closed during the summer** (on side facing the sun) to block the sunlight. You may want to open the window curtains on the shady side of your home. This should help keep the temperature in your home a few degrees lower.

52. **Choose your home repair contractors carefully.** Never make a full payment until the work is completed satisfactorily in full.

53. **Consider planting a tree next to your outside air conditioning unit.** By shading your outside unit you may improve the operating efficiency of the overall system approximately 20%. Be careful not to plant it too close to your unit, as it could restrict proper airflow. You can purchase small trees at your local nursery or discount hardware store.

Food & Household Needs

54. **Be sure to look at the lowest shelves.** When shopping, many times you will find the items with the smallest profit margin on the lower or highest shelves in stores.

55. **Avoid pre-packaged foods.** The little snack packs are convenient, but you can accomplish the same thing for less cost, by buying a larger package of chips or cookies and then

dividing into smaller portions using zip bags. The unit cost savings will help your purse or wallet feel a lot better.

56. **Cook enough for at least two meals.** When you cook lunch or dinner meals, cook enough for two meals. Tomorrow's meal can be leftovers. This will cut the cost of cooking meals for your family.

57. **Grow a few of your own vegetables and nut tree**. A square foot garden can produce enough for some great summer salads without adding to your grocery bill. Also consider planting a pecan tree and if you like grapes, at least two grape vines.

58. **Reduce or say no to fast food**. The cost of fast food can add up. Consider the difference in the cost of a fast food meal for four people versus sandwiches, chips and drinks from home. When traveling, consider bring some of the food from home, and serve it "picnic style" at a public rest area. Your family and mate will probably have more fun in the process.

59. **Coupon deals**. Don't use coupons to buy something you don't need. Many times, you may get a better deal on store brands, even though they don't have a cents-off coupon. Remember to compare the unit cost shelf labels.

60. **Shop at a farmers market for in-season produce**. Few things taste as good as fresh fruits and vegetables. Unfortunately, most of the produce you'll find in a grocery store is grown elsewhere. Help boost the economy in your area by supporting your local growers at the neighborhood farmers market.

61. **Avoid using the oven during the summer**. Ovens heat up a house faster than any other appliance, adding to the strain on air conditioner systems. Plan meals that don't require baking, or bake in the late evening, or use your microwave.

62. **Look for manager specials.** If you buy these items, plan to use them soon because they may have short expiration dates.

63. **Buy generic foods and household supplies where possible**. Forget brand loyalty when trying to save money. The same holds true with other foods and household supplies. When shopping always look for the unit price for the item you are purchasing. There are a few exceptions, but for the most part generic items are just as good as name brands. This includes the medicines, breads, and cereals that you purchase also.

64. **When you eat out pass up on the expensive soft drinks, coffee, and tea**. Ask for water instead. Studies show that most American do not drink a sufficient amounts of water.

65. **Don't be afraid to ask a retailer to match another dealer's price on the same item**. Most major retailers will match the price on like items, rather than lose the sale. Be sure to bring your advertising circular with you as proof of pricing.

66. **When eating out, divide entrees in half and save the rest for a second meal**. Ask for a to-go box as soon as your meal arrives and save half for tomorrow's lunch. This move will help you spread out the calories and cost of the meal. This is not allowed when you eat "buffet style".

67. **Drink less bottled water, drinks, and tea when you eat out.** Drink water when you eat out instead of the expensive drinks that add to the cost of your meal.

68. **Brown bag-it to work.** Can you believe how much a combo meal is at a fast food restaurant? Bring your own soft drinks and snacks to work. Try to avoid the high priced vending snacks and drinks. Buy family-size packaged snacks at the grocery store.

69. **Plan a weekly** menu before shopping and watch your grocery bill shrink. Plan your meals by the week. When you cook, cook enough for two meals.

70. **Don't be blind-sided by familiar product brands**, such as cereals and breads, that usually decrease package sizes while keeping prices constant, a normal industry response to rising food costs.

71. **Be on the alert.** A grocery store's main aisles, like the pathway to milk and bread, are usually strewn with high-priced impulse products. Avoiding those areas will really help your grocery budget.

72. **Shop early in the day.** Instead of following the crowd, beat them there. You get through the store faster with your list and chances are you will spend less. Look for mark downs, and you can save from 10-50% on some items.

73. **Keep your eyes open while shopping so** you can take advantage of in-store coupon displays. Also, remember to clip coupons you need from your local newspaper.

74. **Check online** for your local supermarket's online home page for coupons. It might be a good idea to sign up for any e-mail blasts that are available. **Call products 800 numbers or product websites** for special offers that can be used at your local merchants. A few big box retailers guarantee that if the item doesn't ring up at the correct price, you get it for free or at a discount. Inquire about the store policy where your shop frequently.

75. **Avoid purchasing non-grocery items**, such as painkillers, contact lens solution, etc., at a grocery store. You usually pay more there. Chances are they will cost less at your local discount drug chain store.

76. **If a retailer offers rain checks**, always get a rain check if a sale item is out of stock.

77. **Check your store where their "discounted section is located.** Most have a place set aside where they offer clearance and discounted products.

78. **Shop with a calculator.** Your calculator may come in handy because some stores don't display unit.

79. **Don't assume.** Just because you're in a bargain store doesn't mean you're getting the best price on every item. This applies to the "DOLLAR STORE" concept also. Always compare price and size.

80. **Always check your receipts for accuracy.** No matter how careful you or the store clerks might be; mistakes happen frequently.

81. **Check newspaper advertisements** for the specials at each store where you plan to shop. Remember! Anything that you don't need is not a bargain, no matter how inexpensive it is.

82. **You pay extra for everything they do for you.** Buy unprocessed foods whenever possible.

83. **Shopping can be enjoyable.** Never shop while you are hungry or tired. Stay calm, and resist the urge to be in a hurry.

84. **Consider leaving your kids at home while you shop.** They generally pressure you to buy more than you intended to buy, and may cause you to spend more time shopping than you intended.

85. **Stick to your list.** Don't be tempted to do a lot of browsing. Try to make it a habit of not being in the store for more than 30 minutes.

86. **Test the store brand of your favorite foods.** There are many times when their quality is as good as the national brands. This can add up over a period of time, especially if you frequently purchase this item.

87. **Trim your food bill** a few percentage points by shopping at one or two stores. If you have an advertising circular, circle the items you intend to purchase before you leave to shop.

88. **Carry only the amount you expect to spend at the grocery store.** If you pay cash for your grocery, carry only what you expect to spend, after you have estimated what you intend to spend.

Clothing

89. **Buy wrinkle-free clothes to avoid or reduce your dry cleaning bill.** Avoid buying as many things as possible that requires ironing. You will save in the long run on the time and money spent ironing or dry cleaning.

90. **Buy clothing in the off season.** Most stores usually offer discounts for off season purchases. Many times you can find exceptional values that aren't available in peak season.

91. **Look for kids clothes at yard sales and thrift shops.** Kids have a way of outgrowing most of their clothes before they "out use" them. For this reason, many times you can find excellent buys on clothing at thrift shops and yard sales. Don't forget that you can also pass down clothes from older children if you have any.

92. **Install a clothes line in your back yard.** You will need to purchase clothes pins. Hang your clothes on the line during the warm and mild months. Use your dryer during the winter months. This will help lower your utility bill.

93. **Wash clothes in the cold water cycle.** Hot water is a significant part of your electric bill.

94. **Use a drying rack or line dry heavy clothing.** If you live in an apartment complex, you may want to consider purchasing a drying rack to dry heavy garments and towels. When nearly dry, place your heavy clothes in the dryer with a dryer sheet for just a few minutes to complete the drying cycle, remove wrinkles, and soften clothes.

95. **Buy clothes after the Christmas season or the off season.** Most stores will markdown certain merchandise after the holiday season. Visit the websites of stores you wish to shop. Most of them will offer you an opportunity to register so they can send you e-mails when they are having specials throughout the year.

Medical

96. **Ask your doctor to consider prescribing generic drugs** instead of the higher priced brand names.

97. **If you can't afford health insurance.** It is important to have access to health care. Keep in mind, that your local government usually provides free or low cost health care. Contact your local health care for program eligibility requirements.

98. **Reduce or quit smoking.** Smoking has been proven to be an unhealthy habit, and is costly in many ways. If you can't find any other reason to quit, think about your health, finances, and all the people that love and admire you.

Recreation

99. **Reduce trips to the theater or skip the theater, subscribe to Netflix or another online rental source.** Going to the movie theater is a great way to beat the heat, but it's also expensive. Skip the theater, and sign up for an online DVD rental service. You don't have to worry about late fees, and look at the valuable time you saved.

100. **Share DVD's with your relatives or friends.** If you know someone who would be willing to alternate the purchasing and sharing of DVD's, you may be able to save quite a bit of money, and still enjoy the latest movie releases.

101. **Check out the "Dollar stores".** They often carry a few older, but good movies that you probably have not seen. Sometimes, they will have them at 2/$1.00.

102. **Give yourself a raise and save the difference.** Instead of getting a large income tax return, you may choose to maximize your taxable deductions instead of getting a larger refund at tax time. Check with your employer on how to increase your tax exemptions.

103. **Treat your savings plan as if it was a bill.** Treat savings as you would other bills that you have. Consider this a sacrifice, so you will be able to live better later.

104. **Plan your savings to include purchases** you would like to make, instead of buying them on credit. Calculate how much and how long it would take you to save for a particular item. Deposit this amount regularly in your savings account until you have the amount you need to purchase the item.

105. **Save "windfall or found" money in a separate account.** As with any income above your normal earnings, bank the amount in a separate checking or savings account. Use the money to pay down debt, build up savings, or offset unexpected expenses. Some examples are: overtime, tax refunds, stimulus checks, gifts and similar windfalls should be deposited in this account.

106. **Start your own "keep the change" program.** Several banks are now running "keep the change" promotions where they round up your purchases and put the difference in a savings account. The problem is, these accounts normally don't pay a great interest rate, and may encourage increased spending. Create your own program by spending only cash and dumping the change in a coin jar. Make deposits into your own interest-bearing savings account at the end of the month.

107. **Stay clear of your 401k savings plan.** It is almost never a good idea to remove money from your 401k savings plan. If you don't have a life or death situation, your money needs to stay put.

Credit cards and other debts

108. **Avoid convenience checks issued by credit card companies.** They are really cash advances that come with extra fees, and usually have high interest rates than purchases. Your best course of action would probably be to shred them immediately before temptation takes over.

109. **Avoid "payment holidays".** Credit companies usually offer these near the Thanksgiving and Christmas holidays. Remember that interest will accrue on the unpaid balance, even if you don't make an additional purchase.

110. **Don't accept credit line increases unless you need it.** Many lenders will view this as potential debt. Contact your credit company if you don't desire a higher credit limit.

111. **Always pay more than the minimum due on debts that accrue interest.** Always pay more than the minimum amount due on your credit, even if it's only a dollar. The main thing is that you develop a habit of paying more than the minimum. You will be able to increase the amounts you pay later.

112. **Put away the credit cards.** Save cash for large purchases by creating a dedicated savings account specifically for the next item on your list. Make regular contributions to the savings account with each paycheck, and when the balance is high enough to pay for the item, pay for it with cash. Leave your credit cards at home unless you are out of town on

a trip. If something always happens that causes you to keep buying on credit, cut up your credit cards as a last resort.

113. **Ask creditors to lower your interest rate.** Creditors are feeling the crunch, too, and they recognize it takes more money to find a new customer than to retain a current one. If you are a profitable customer (pay interest), call creditors and ask for a lower rate. As your credit improves you should make a request at least once a year if you still have a balance.

114. **Divide credit card minimum payments in half and pay that amount twice a month.** Interest is calculated based on the average daily balance of your account for the entire month. By making a payment every couple weeks you are reducing that average balance and therefore reducing the finance charges assessed, as opposed to waiting until the end of the month to make a single payment. You should be able to do this online. This might not be a good idea unless you are able to do this online.

115. **Transfer existing balances.** Moving existing balances to 0% interest plans helps more of your payment go towards repaying the balance, and less towards interest. Many companies will offer 0% offers for a period of 12 months. During this period pay as much as possible toward the principal. Beware of high upfront fees and go-to rates when considering your options. Make sure the card you are transferring to, has a fixed rate of interest lower than the one you have.

116. **Commit to no new debt.** In order to catch up you have to make a commitment to have "no new debt", by restricting access and temptation to make new debt.

117. **Call your credit card company at least once a year and request a lower interest rate.** This can help you pay down debt faster.

118. **Do you have any assets that can be sold?** Consider a yard sale to help pay off smaller bills. You may even consider selling your boat, extra car, or jewelry to help pay off debts.

119. **Request cancellation of late fees.** If you are late with a payment, call your credit card issuer and request cancellation or reduction of the late fee. If you have not been late in the last 12 months, there is a very good chance they will honor your request.

Taxes

120. **There is great tax return software on the market.** If you have a simple return, consider doing your own tax return. Tax software makes it simple, even if you have a small business. Be sure to save most of the money you would normally spend getting your tax return done.

121. **Adjust your W-4 at work.** If you received a huge refund this year, consider increasing the number of exemptions on your W-4 to reduce withholdings. Check the IRS website to calculate the number of exemptions required to break even (irs.gov). You must contact your employer to add exemptions to your W-4.

122. **Consider setting up a 529 education plan for your children.** The funds withdrawn for this account are usually tax free if they are used for education related expenses.

123. **Consider starting a business** to increase your income and reduce your tax obligations. Remember, keep it simple and fun.

124. **Starting an IRA account** will help you delay some tax liability, while preparing for retirement.

General or Miscellaneous

125. **Eliminating or reducing non-essentials for a while.** All it takes is a little thought and creativity. You may want to subscribe to our monthly "Tips and Advice" newsletter, so you can stay abreast of the latest information. E-mail us at Lawrence.surles@yahoo.com for FREE SAMPLE.

126. **Track expenses** so you will know when you are spending more than what you make.

127. **Paying on time or early is the best way to pay.** Always pay on time, or ahead to avoid late charges. Always pay by the least expensive way possible (in most cases by automatic bank draft or online). By far, these methods of payment have proven to be the most reliable.

128. **Don't buy things just because they are cute.** Reduce excessive gadget spending and other frivolous spending.

129. **Plan for emergencies.** It is a good idea to work toward having at least 30 days of dry and can goods in reserve for storms and emergencies. Don't forget the candles, bottled water, flashlights, and batteries.

130. **Know the life expectancy of high dollar purchases.** Get the maximum useful life of a product that you own so you don't have to replace them prematurely. Follow the maintenance guide for products that you purchase. In plain words, take good care of the things you already have.

131. **Reduce waste and excess in all areas.** Identifying areas of waste. This can help lower expenses, so you can pay more on bills that you wish to pay off.

132. **Look for a value internet package.** If you don't use the internet much, call your provider for any unadvertised viewing packages. If they think that you are going to cancel, you will be surprised at the deals they are willing to offer. They have been known to offer several "free or discounted" months of service to keep you from canceling your service.

133. **Have a no-spend weekend.** Sometimes it takes a break in the routine to get spending under control. Try to go an entire weekend without shopping, or ordering something online. It won't solve all your spending problems, but it's a start. You may even consider camping out in your backyard.

134. **Don't run water when shaving or brushing teeth.** While shaving pull up the sink stopper and pool a little water in the sink for rinsing your razor. You will be surprised at the amount of water used just to do this small chore.

135. **Don't run water to rinse your dishes.** Fill the sink with water instead.

136. **Bathe your own pets.** Skip the pet grooming salon, pickup some shampoo at a pet supply store and wash them yourself. Why miss all the fun?

137. **Weekend or Sunday paper only.** Consider scaling back subscriptions such as newspapers to the bare minimum. Most people don't have the time to read the newspaper everyday. Call your carrier to see if you can get Saturday and Sunday only.

138. **Don't renew the gym membership.** Being healthy can save you money, but fees and inflexible contracts make gyms a burden on your budget. Take the money you would have spent at the gym and try to build one at home for the whole family. All it takes is a little creativity and you can still get "gym quality" results. If you have a fairly safe neighborhood, running in pairs with your spouse or neighbor would be a good idea.

139. **Make home birthday cakes.** Your child will be just as happy, because they will know that it was an expression of your love for them.

140. **Discover your local library.** To replace the time previously spent watching television develop a reading habit, and support your local library while you are at it. Can't find the book you are looking for? Don't rush out and buy it. Many times libraries are networked and can request a copy of a book from another library. You may be able to reserve books, DVD's, and CD's on the internet. Most libraries also rent DVD's and CD's at little or no charge.

141. **Bring you lawn hose in for the winter.** This will prolong the life of your water hose. This also applies to you lawn mower, and other tools you might leave outside during the winter.

142. **Don't pay for banking privileges.** There are too many free checking options out there to pay one penny in fees for the right to write a check or use a debit card. Many banks and credit unions simply require direct deposit or a minimum number of debit card uses per month to qualify for fee-free accounts. Call around town for the best deal and convenience that fits your lifestyle.

143. **Buy generic ink cartridges for your printer.** Check out a generic cartridge reseller. The quality of ink is comparable to manufacturer's ink, and many may offer a dollar or two off if you recycle the old cartridge.

144. **Read family magazines, etc.** You should be able to find ideas about how to have more fun with your family and friends while staying at home. You can pick up hints on how to organize recreation activities for the family. You can read many of these at your local library. You may also check out the website of your favorite magazines.

145. **Cross train at work to make yourself more valuable.** This is especially good if the position you are cross-training for pays more. Make yourself more layoff-proof with this new skill.

146. **Let your tailgate down.** If you drive a truck, you could let your tailgate down. Tests and experiments have shown this to be only a slight contribution to reduce your gas expense.

147. **If you pay extra for long distance calls.** Try to keep you calls short and to the point. Even though we have cell phones, it's nice, and rather heart warming to send a letter every now and then.

148. **Make some gifts sometimes instead of making more purchases.** It is the thought behind the gift that counts. So put your creativity to work.

149. **Consider a roommate if you are single.** You can use some of this money to pay off smaller bills, or perhaps save 10 percent. If you decide to take in a roommate, a good suggestion is to stick with the same sex.

150. **Consider a part time job.** Use the extra income to accelerate payments on your smallest <u>closed end</u> bill. Don't spend the extra money just because you have it. A closed end bill is one that you can't add any more debt to it.

151. **Have a block put on your cell phone for text messages.** Unwanted and unsolicited text messages can add up over time. A call to your carrier's customer service department may eliminate this lesser priority expense. Carriers don't normally block them unless you request it.

152. **Cancel or down-size your satellite or cable TV viewing packages.** Consider canceling or scaling back to only the basic channels for a while. You could also consider purchasing one or two DVD's monthly instead, which should result in substantial savings.

153. **Consider bartering or trading for goods and services you need.** Many businesses and individuals are willing to trade most anything from printing, meals, lawn services, advertising space, computer services and much more. Check the yellow pages under "bartering".

154. **Cut your own hair.** If you or someone in your home is handy with clippers, you may be able to look good and lower your monthly expenses at the same time. It works for me!

155. **You'll be surprised at the things you can live without.** If you have a problem with impulse spending, you could practice waiting at least 24 hours before making your purchase. This can be especially useful when deciding to purchase something on credit.

156. **Paint your own fingernails.** You can do this instead of paying for a manicure.

157. **Mow your own yard.** This can replace exercise from time to time.

158. **Start shopping early for Christmas.** If you are planning to buy gifts for Christmas, estimate the amount you expect to spend, and include this amount in your savings plan, so you will not have to buy on credit.

159. **Don't try to live the lifestyle of the rich and famous.** The glitter of the bling-bling can prove to be an unnecessary weight on your budget.

160. **Plan for upcoming expenses.** Take time to consider, and plan for any major expense for the upcoming months. Determine how much you will have to save to cover these future expenses.

161. **Search for an airline that let kids travel for free.** Book your flight early for the best discounts.

162. **Search for hotels that let kids stay free.** This is one of the many things hotels use to entice travelers to stay. Inquire if they offer "free continental breakfast" also.

163. **Cancel any unused magazine subscriptions.** You can subscribe to them later if you desire, or you can read them for free at your local library.

164. **Consider buying some used clothing,** instead of new all the time.

165. **Be willing to forego the purchase of designer name brand clothing** for a while. Many up and coming brands offer clothing with comparable value.

166. **Provide for kids within the limits of your income.** Don't use money as a substitute for spending quality time with your kids.

167. **If you receive the Sunday newspaper,** save the comic page to wrap gifts for Christmas and other occasions.

168. **Pass up on the designer checks.** They normally cost more than plain checks.

169. **Most microwave ovens use less energy than conventional ovens** and they usually cook food much faster. Think of the things you can accomplish with the time and money you save.

170. **Keep you home comfortable.** In the summer time set your thermostat to 78 degrees. In the winter, in the winter, 73 degrees.

171. **Be sure to turn off televisions,** stereos, and computers when they will not be in use for extended periods of time.

172. **Use a timer to turn security lights on and off** while you are away from home, or you may want to consider a security light with a built-in motion detector.

173. **Open an account at a bank or credit union that does not charge a fee** to maintain your account. Some institutions may require a certain amount to be deposited in order to not be charge fees.

174. **Consider paying some bills on auto-pay** to save on postage, time, etc. You won't have to worry about your bills not being paid on time. Consider working toward putting all your bills on auto pay.

175. **Review your expense summary** and look for other areas in which you can cut for a while. Get a sheet of paper. Most people have 10 -25 bills or expenses. Write the name of each expense at the top of the page. Number each line on the paper from 1-22. On each line write down things you can do to reduce this expense. Draw a line through each of your ideals as you execute them.

176. **Be careful about seeking another full-time income.** If your family can cover expenses with one income, you shouldn't seek a second income merely to increase income, unless you have a definite plan. When you consider the extra expenses of a second job, it may not be worth it… taxes, childcare, transportation, and strained relationships.

177. **Attend local High school games.** Usually they are less expensive than College or Pro games.

178. **Get free long distance on your computer.** Check out this website. Magic jack.com.

179. **Bundle your phone with your cable and internet for a lower overall rate.** Many companies offer lower rates when you use more than one of the services they offer.

180. **Turn off unnecessary features.** Stick with the pre-installed ring tones instead of downloading new ones. You should start to see a reduction in your cell phone bill. You can find free ring tones on the internet.

181. **Get directory assistance for Free.** You can use these numbers from a cellular or landline phone. 1-800-466-4411 or 1-800-373-3411.

182. **Live one pay raise below.** Save the difference. Don't be so quick to start spending more because you got a pay raise. You can choose to pay the extra income on your debts, if you have any.

183. **E-mail us for the latest FREE UPDATED COPY** of this SUGGESTION CHECKLIST at least every six months. Lawrence.surles@yahoo.com

You can find more ways to lower your expenses

Count all you bills. _You will need a sheet of note book paper, or you may choose to make a copy of this page for each bill you have._ Example: One sheet for your electric bill, one sheet for food, one sheet for you house payment, Direct TV, and so on. Below is an example sheet.

Name of this bill is

_____

Note: Write down as many ideas that you can think of to lower this bill. **Write it down even if it does not make sense right at this moment.** You can line it out later if you choose. If you are using the "envelope system, you may want to attach this to the bill it pertains to.

Date due _____Minimum payment due $_____

Account balance $ _____Variable or fixed bill. Circle one.

Line out or put a check mark beside each step as you implement it

Pay Period Cash Flow Chart

Use one of these each time you receive a paycheck or income. This chart is configured for people who get paid twice monthly. Feel free to customize it to fit your needs.

Today's payday – Date _____

My/our take home pay after taxes is $_____.

My next pay day is – Date _____.My beginning checking account balance is $ _____.

My list of all bills due, or expenses that will be paid out this pay period.

Bills that are due this pay period (You may round off if you choose). Show how you will pay it: cash, check, debit, bank draft, money order, etc.

Date Due	Description of bill	Amount Due	How you pay it

My ending balance in my check book should be $ _____.

ANNUAL INCOME & EXPENSE FLOW CALENDAR

Month	Actual Income	Expenses	Short/Over
January			
February			
March			
April			
May			
June			
July			
August			
September			
October			
November			
December			
Annual Totals $	$	$	

List twelve ways you can entertain yourself, your family and friends for less than you are currently doing for the next twelve months.

Schedule your ideas throughout your "Things to do list".

CHAPTER SEVEN
CONNECTING TO SUPPORT SYSTEMS

CHAPTER SEVEN OBJECTIVES: The objective of this chapter is to connect you with people, businesses, and organizations that can provide information or other assistance to help you reach your goals. You can do this by attending functions where you are likely to meet people whose interests are similar to yours. You may also find many social networking sites online.

Home	Keep up with current events and other information that can be helpful to you.
Church	There may be members in your church that can assist you with some, or all of the information you need.
Government	Local, State, and National government offer may programs to help improve the life and skills of its citizens.
Non -profits	You should be able to find a local non-profit that is doing community work that interests you.
Internet	The internet is great place to search for information on almost any subject matter.
Workshops	Many times local businesses offer free or low cost workshops on subjects that may interest you.
Continuing Education Classes	Many area community colleges offer continuing education classes for adults. Many also offer online classes.
Social Networking	You can do this by attending functions where you are likely to meet people whose interests are similar to yours. You may also find many social networking sites online.
Other	

CHECK OUT THESE WEBSITES
(You may be able find information that can be helpful to you)

Free Annual Credit Reports	Annualcreditreports.com1-877-322-8228
TransUnion Credit Reporting Agency	1-800-888-4213
FIOC Scores	Myfico.com
Federal Trade Commission	Ftc.gov
National Foundation for Consumer Credit	1-800-388-2227
Veterans Administration Benefits	1-800-827-1000
Social Security Administration	1-800-827-1213
Freddie Mac Budget Calculators	freddiemac.com/calculators
Prevent foreclosures	1-888-995-HOPE
To remove your name from pre-screened mailing lists	www.optoutprescreen.com 1(888) 567-8688
National Do Not Call Registry	www.donotcall.gov 1-888-382-1222
Internal Revenue Service	Irs.gov
Federal Deposit Insurance (check here for current banking coverage limits	Fdic.gov
Community Service Volunteers	Usaservice.org

To receive an updated copy of this list or any questions concerning this book, you can E-mail us at: Lawrence.surles@yahoo.com

CHAPTER EIGHT
ORGANIZING YOUR AFFAIRS FOR ONGOING GROWTH AND MATURITY

CHAPTER EIGHT OBJECTIVES: We hope to assist you in setting up your affairs so they can benefit you and the next generations.

Know what success means to you

- **Be careful who you allow to determine what success means to you.** Never allow anyone to measure your success in dollars and cents. Make extra effort to garnish the skills that you are naturally gifted in.
- You must be the one to decide what things are important to you, and will make your life more meaningful.
- Assess the potential risks and rewards when making decisions. When you realize that you have made a mistake, learn from it, and be determined not to repeat it again.
- Shy away from situations where the risks far outweigh the potential rewards, such as gambling and lotteries.

Schedule your daily tasks

- Get organized. Make your schedule the day, or night before.
- List your daily tasks by time to be completed. Circle the most important ones. **You should focus on the important tasks first; complete them before going to the next tasks.** Keep it simple and systematic. Break hard projects into steps, such as using a checklist for each step. Communicate often with your spouse so both will know where assistance is needed.
- Learn to delegate certain tasks to free up your time to be productive in areas of more importance, such as automatic draft for automatic savings and investing.

Learning to recognize upward trends and traditional things that hold value for investment possibilities in tough times

- Water
- Electric
- Energy
- Medical
- Alternate clean energy
- Municipal bonds
- Treasury or Saving bonds

Seek to stabilize your income, savings and investments

- Pay yourself (save and invest a portion of all income you receive). Start with your emergency fund first, then when it is adequate, start setting aside for retirement and other investing.
- As you pay down your debts, increase your savings to at least 10% of the payment you where making.
- Pre-pay certain bills to create flexibility in your budget.
- Plan for emergencies (death, job loss, flat tires, auto maintenance, etc.)
- Any time you have automatic deductions from your payroll check or checking accounts for savings and investments, you will increase your chances of being able to stick with your plans and obtain your goals.
- Organize, but keep it simple.
- Schedule your main daily tasks by priority and time.
- Open retirement accounts. Use your payroll deductions to your advantage.
- If you must borrow, borrow from yourself. You will normally get a lower interest rate.
- Reinvest for a higher yield, such as a CD. You can use the internet to shop banks for the highest CD yield within your State.
- Once you pay off a bill, start paying most of that bill to yourself in the form of savings.
- Consider selling some of the things you don't need. Anytime you are going to make a purchase, carefully consider if you will be able to afford the maintenance on this item.
- Use your payroll deductions to your advantage so that you can make sure you have enough deducted to cover your tax obligations without giving the government a free loan for the year.
- Limit the amount that you borrow. Be realistic, if you don't have a good feeling about borrowing a certain amount of money, don't do it.
- Be persistent, but know when to quit. Set limits as to the amount of time, energy, and resources you are willing to risk to accomplish a particular goal.
- Learn to delegate certain tasks to free up your time.
- Reduce the clutter and distractions.
- Learn to leverage your time, energy, and resources.
- **Consider the "rule of 72" when it comes to investing.** The "rule of 72" is the methods used to determine how long it would take for a one-time invest to double at a certain rate. Example: Divide 72 by the rate of return. 72 divided by 5.0 rate of return = 14.6 years. Ask your banker to explain this to you.

Preparing for the unexpected and emergencies

- Auto- Always carry such things a flashlight, batteries, life vest, tools in your car.
- Home – Secondary heating method in case of an extend power outage, such as a kerosene heater.
- Work-Know the procedure for calling in late for work. Keep it handy in your wallet.

Basic General Savings Guidelines.

A good rule of thumb is to save (liquid) three to six months of living expenses. Put one to two months of savings into a savings account, and six months or more into certificates of deposits (CD) as a reserve. If you are self-employed you should reserve at least twice that amount. A good plan is to have a system of automatic savings that can replenish the account in case you have to use some of it. Although three to six months is the ideal cushion, it won't happen instantly. Take small steps, it's going to take quite a while to save that amount of money. ***Start building your savings regularly.***

_____ Open a checking account
_____ Open a savings account
_____ Open a Certificate of Deposit.
_____ Set up and contribute automatically to your retirement accounts each paycheck.
_____ Investigate other investments to supplement and eventually replace your current income.

*Automate your savings as soon as you have a positive cash flow and emergency fund in place.

Your children and the importance of savings

Now is a good time to introduce your child to the benefits of saving. Here are some tips to help teach young children the importance of smart money habits:

Offering them an allowance for the things they do gives them their first taste of financial freedom. **Opening a bank account** is a good way to introduce children to the concept of saving. Encourage them to divide up their money: Money they can spend now, some for charity, and savings for their goals. Assist them in setting up their own savings account. Take them to the bank regularly. Assist them with their savings transactions until they understand what to do. Consider starting a 529 college savings plan in their early years.

Wealth Creation

1. Start saving early, save regularly. Pay into it on time, as you would any other bill you are responsible for. Re-invest most or all of your earnings.
2. Set a minimum to goal to save at least 10% or more of your gross income.
3. Expand your portfolio through long term growth over a long period of time.
4. Purchase or leverage income producing assets or assets which tend to increase in value, instead of purchasing liabilities.
5. Position yourself for residual income, such as with business ownership.
6. Spend time tuning up your skills and level of training in areas that interest you.
7. Volunteer some of your time, resources, and talents to benefit others.
8. Understand that time is valuable when it comes to compound interest accrued on your money. If you manage your time well, you can accumulate enough money, so you can pay for another person's time.
9. Spend less than what you earn. If what you have coming in continues to be less than what you got going out, then your upkeep will be your downfall. You will never be able to create any real wealth.

10. Make sure your income and assets are diversified to reduce the impact of planned and unanticipated risks.
11. Learn and teach yourself and your next generation asset management principles.
12. Make sure you have a valid will in place to facilitate to reduce the risks associated with the transfer of wealth to the next generation.

Example of how your savings can grow:

- Use pre-tax deductions such as a company profit sharing plan.
- Include extra savings to your emergency savings account.
- Create a separate side savings account with the express purpose of meeting your tax bill.
- Incorporate the added savings into your regular monthly budget so that while you may only pay taxes or insurance once a year, you are effectively breaking the bill into 12 smaller chunks.

<u>*Look at this example of compound interest:*</u>

Let's assume that you can save $100 per month, and your savings will earn 8%. Keep in mind that these figures do not include factors such as market conditions, taxes, inflation, or other variables.

10 years	$ 17,680
20 years	56,923
30 years	$144,028
40 years	$337,371

Marks of maturity

- Your money should be working hard for you. Automatic re-investment is essential. Re-invest any profits you make. Sure, it normally takes money to make money, but that does not mean you have to have a lot to start.
- Your bills and personal matters are organized so that the tasks of managing your affairs are fast, more efficient, pleasant, in most instances.
- Your budget is organized so your spending plan covers all your bills, and helps you be prepared to cover them if your current income does not meet your current expenses.
- Unselfishness. Be willing to help others in need, without expecting something in return.
- You do not show partially in your business and personal dealings. Be fair to everyone.
- You should not take undue risks, so you can keep the potential for losses low.

Seek professional advice from time to time.

This is your opportunity to get a second opinion and professional guidance. We suggest you do this at a minimum, once a year. This way, you get a chance to get guidance from someone who knows this field, so you can ultimately make better decisions.

- **Start your own business.**

If you are waiting to inherit a lot of money, your chances are slim. Having your own business is the number one way to increase income, create wealth and lower taxes. E-mail us **Lawrence.surles@yahoo.com,** and request FREE INFORMATION on a great business opportunity that will compliment almost any career field.

Set up an orderly transfer of wealth to help provide financial security for future generations:

1. Review your will and other important documents annually to make sure they are up to date.
2. Set up a trust account for your grandchildren when they are born.
3. Make sure someone knows where you keep your important papers. Don't let your death become a problem for your loved ones.

If you must borrow:

- Always have a several ways out if the situation goes sour.
- If you must borrow, secure your own debt if possible.
- Make sure the rate is reasonable.
- Be willing to walk away from a deal that is not in your best interest.
- Purchase something that will increase your income or increase in value over the years.
- Secure the loan. Usually secured loans are charged less interest than unsecured loans.

CHAPTER NINE
CREATING CUSHIONS TO REDUCE UNNECESSARY RISKS

Chapter Objectives: Our aim is to help you shield your assets from unnecessary risks, and reduce or eliminate the stress of money shortage challenges. We will suggest the diversification of assets, and risk deduction in all areas. We hope to help you be prepared for emergencies, rather than using more credit financing to make up shortages, that actually keeps you in debt.

Checking Account

Shop around for a good bank or credit union that offers free checking, even if you have to maintain a certain account balance for free checking. Some will even offer to pay interest on your account balance. If you are married, be sure to have at least one joint checking account. It would be helpful if you can access your accounts via the internet.

Emergency savings accounts

This is your reserve account in the event of a foreseen emergency. Don't "put in and take out": this is a savings account, not a checking account. Don't touch it unless you truly have an emergency. Maintain funds for periodic bills, vacations and fun activities in a separate account. People without emergency funds tend to live in debt and paycheck to paycheck. You should first accumulate money in an emergency fund before you start investing. This is an important step in starting a workable savings plan that can help you reach your immediate, midterm, and long term goals. This will serve as your liquid account; a regular savings account is sufficient for this purpose. You must be able to access this account on any normal banking day. This will help shield you from the stress of not being able to cover most unexpected expenses. Do not keep this money in your checking account, or in an account connected to your checking account. This money should be in a separate, interest bearing account. If you have to, you may want to put this money in another bank you don't use frequently. We suggest that you have no more than one (1) month salary in this account. Any amount above one months' salary should be placed into CD's when you accumulate enough money. It would be a good idea to have the amount you intend to save automatically deducted. Think of all the stress that you will eliminate because you have the foresight to plan ahead. This account will allow you to have a reserve for the surprises that are sure to come. This will also help you cover the periodic bills that will be coming due at various times of the year. An emergency fund will prove to be valuable if your paycheck varies. You will be able to pay your bills, even when your paycheck occasionally comes up short. Saving for emergencies doesn't have to be about painful cutbacks or inflexible spending measures. Sometimes we get so focused on where we're going to find extra money that we forget the small things we can do to build our savings. We suggest some of the following strategies: *As you pay off your debts, keep increasing the amount you are paying yourself by saving and investing.*

Getting the best use for the money you have earned

1. If you are going to buy any impulse gadgets, wait at least 24 hours before making the purchase.
2. Plan your spending, make budgeting fun and interesting. Reward and celebrate yourself in a small way each time you reach one of your goals.
3. Keep your regular savings and emergency fund account separate, even if you have to open an account at another bank.
4. Be serious about saving regularly. Treat it as though it was a bill or taxes you need to pay. Don't carry large amounts of cash; it's better off in the bank so it can be working for you.
5. **If you are expecting a tax return, you may want to use a portion of it to establish an emergency fund.**
6. Don't be tempted to spend your money. Always re-invest most of your profits. Do something nice for someone, or help someone that is in need.

Certificate of Deposits (CD)

Usually you can purchase these at your local financial institution. They will allow you to earn a higher rate of return than your regular savings account. They also are less liquid, meaning you can't cash them out tomorrow without being penalized. They are normally available for deposits starting at six months or more. Interest rates paid on CD's change periodically. *You should not purchase one of these until you have your emergency fund in place.*

Employer 401k and profit sharing plans

Check with your employer for any retirement or profit sharing plans they may offer.

Mutual Fund Accounts

Make regular savings contributions to this account, preferably by payroll deduction. This may vary in value from time to time, but you should look at this as a long term investment historically should increase in value over a long period of time. Contact your credit union, bank, or financial advisor for details.

Automotive Insurance

For example, if you owned a new auto and a 3-4 year old auto, you would be able to reduce your insurance premiums because of the age of the second car. Consider increasing your insurance deductible when you have enough to cover it in your emergency fund, or other accounts.

Alternate solution to the high cost of health insurance:

It is not a wise idea to be without medical coverage. Although health insurance is expensive, you can't afford to be without some type of coverage. It only takes one doctor bill to wipe out a life time of savings.

You may qualify for an affordable, biblical alternative to expensive health care insurance that could save you $2,000 to $4,000 a year or more. Medi-Share, a not-for-profit ministry, provides biblically based, non-insurance healthcare solution for many Christian families. Their mission is simple: Enable Christians to greatly reduce the cost of their healthcare- without reducing the quality-by sharing their medical bills with one another. They were organized in 1993, and have gown to over 60,000 members in all 50 states. You may call them at: 1-800-772-5623, or visit there website at www.medi-share.org.

Reducing risks by getting control of your credit cards:

- In most cases you should only have two to three credit cards. You don't have to close the accounts, but you can cut the cards up.
- Don't use your credit card as though it was a savings account.
- Don't treat your credit card as though it was additional income.
- Don't wait until the date due to pay. Don't make late payments, even if you have to pay early. At some point, you should consider auto draft for your payments. Now you should never have to worry about the harassing phone calls and late fees.
- Negotiate for a lower rate at least once a year if you have a balance that can't be paid in full when due.
- Don't share your credit with anyone: (Example: Mother, sister, brother)
- Don't hide your debt from your spouse. Always consult your mate before making large purchases (for example: consult your spouse before any purchase over $150).
- Restrict access to new debt. This will lessen the temptation to acquire new debt. Cut up the cards, but don't cancel them yet.
- Don't use cash advances to pay off other loans, unless your card has a fixed rate of interest that is lower than what you are paying on the other loan. Many companies have a transaction charge. Normally this is between 2-3 % of the amount advanced.
- If you are divorced, you may want to close joint accounts. By law merchants cannot close a joint account because of martial status, but can do so at the request of either spouse. For more information, log on to FTC.gov.

Increase your credit score and build your credit rating to help you qualify for necessary loans and, even save thousands in interest charges.

- Always pay on time, or ahead of time. The most efficient way to pay your bills may be to have them drafted from your checking account.
- Keep your balance low compared to your credit limit. Catch up on past due accounts.
- Apply for credit only when you need it.
- Use idle accounts that report to the credit reporting agencies at least once a year to keep them active for credit reference purposes.
- Monitor your credit reports often, and check for errors and outdated entries.
- **Know the Federal limits of liabilities in the event of loss or theft.**
- Start making arrangements to start paying or settling old debts.
- Report any problems with your account to the card company.
- Never loan anyone your card or borrow for others on your card.
- Don't cosign for others. Co-signing for the debts of others who would not normally qualify is a personal choice, and is very risky in most cases. If the loan company sees them as risky, why shouldn't you also. Many friendships have been shivered as a result of co-signing for debts.

Smart ways to use your tax refund is:

- Get current on past due bills.
- Start or increase your emergency fund.
- If you are barely breaking even on your budget, pay certain bills ahead, such as electric, water, or telephone. This should lower your monthly bills for a while and reduce the excess stress of barely having enough to pay bills.
- Save a majority of your refund as part of your emergency fund; next focus the remaining on paying down your debt.
- Make needed repairs and maintenance on your transportation to work. This may help prevent a lot of surprises because of unexpected expenses.

Identity Theft

At this point identity theft is the fast growing crime in the USA. It is a very serious crime. It occurs when your personal information is stolen by various means without your consent. Thieves can steal information about you by rummaging through your trash, stealing your card number by using a special storage device when processing your card, or even putting in a change of address, and diverting your mail to another address. There are number of ways to deter identity thieves by safeguarding your information in the following ways:

- Do not have your social security number printed on your checks. Do not write your social security number on checks that you write.
- Never click on unsolicited e-mails.
- Be sure to keep your personal information at home in a safe and secure place, or in a safe deposit box at your local financial institution.
- Always shred documents with personal information before you place them in the trash can.
- Never give out personal information on the phone to unsolicited offers.
- Contact creditors of any accounts you suspect to have been tampered with.
- When using your computer, never use obvious passwords, such as the last 4 of your social security number, your mothers' maiden name, and your birthday.
- Review your financial statements when they arrive, looking for charges you did not make or authorize.
- Be sure to get free credit reports annually. You may do this by calling 1-877-322-8228, or online at www.annualcreditreport.com.
- Check out any letters or, calls concerning purchases that you did not make. If you suspect identity theft, file a report with you local police. You should also file a report with Federal Trade Commission (FTC.gov/idtheft). You may also reach the FTC by calling 1-877-438-4338, or TTY, 1-866-653-4261
- If you suspect fraud, you should contact the credit reporting companies and have fraud alert placed on your account. When you place a fraud alert at the credit reporting companies you may be entitled to free credit report. The three major credit reporting companies are: EQUIFAX 1-800-525-6285, EXPERIAN 1-888-397-3742, and TRANSUNION 1-800-680-7289.
- To learn more about how you can protect your credit rating, go to FTC.gov

Your bank and your money

Is your money safe?

What's covered by Federal Deposit Insurance Corporation (FDIC)?

Currently the FDIC insures up to $250,000 on certain retirement accounts. Coverage for general accounts is $100,000. Coverage amount may be adjusted to reflect inflation. Check FDIC.gov for the most current coverage amounts. Also inquire at your financial institution as to whether they are a member of the FDIC.

- Negotiable Order of withdrawal, or NOW, accounts
- Checking accounts
- Savings, Money Market, and Certificates of Deposits (CD's)

What's not covered by FDIC?

- Bonds, Mutual Funds, and Stocks
- The contents of your safe deposit box
- Treasury securities and savings bonds (Investment secured by the US Government.
- Annuity and Insurance products
- Losses due to theft or fraud at your institution. These situations are normally covered by insurance policies that financial institutions purchase from private insurance carriers.

CHAPTER TEN

INCREASING OR REPLACING YOUR INCOME

CHAPTER TEN OBJECTIVES: Our aim is to help you leverage assets to provide income so you can enjoy your golden years, provide income when you are unable to work, against possible job loss, and help .provide a financial foundation for future generations.

Why increase or replace your current income?

- You will have increased flexibility of how you choose to spend your time.
- You will have income even if you lose your job.
- Income for the times when you are unable to work, or to leave a financial foundation for the next generation.

Note: For the sake of this book our definition of wealth is: How long you can pay your bills if you received no income from your job.

You could be preparing for the golden years (retirement) and possible job loss.

- Mutual Funds- This should be considered a long term investment. Your risk of loss is reduced by spreading your money among various investments. This is called diversification. There is still no guarantee that your investments won't suffer if the market drops, but it can improve your chances of losing all your money.

Time Freedom

- Your assets work for you instead of you working for them. Having money and having wealth is two different concepts. You can pay bills with money you earn at work, but wealth can pay bills when you don't work
- Consistent savings is essential to financial freedom.
- Consider relationship marketing for income and tax advantages.
- Search for things that increase in value with time to keep pace with inflation.
- Get acquainted with the "investment triangle." Talk to your financial advisor, bank, or search online the investment triangle concept. The idea is to investment more in saving, CD's, Mutual funds, and so on. And less in speculative investments such as stock purchases.

Tips and hints to help you build wealth and give yourself a raise:

1. Be sure you save a portion of any income that you receive, to include raises, tax refunds, and bonuses. It is necessary that you save regularly and consistently to build your savings. Don't be afraid to ask for help and advice. But, keep in mind that the decision how you use information you receive is your responsibility.

2. Use your time wisely: Family time, and study time. Keep up with current events. Limit the amount of time you and your family play video games.
3. Try to get the best return on investment, with the least possible risks.
4. Weigh the risks and rewards of each investment.
5. Don't assume you can't invest because your credit is bad.
6. Diversify your investments to spread the risk and impact of losses.
7. It is important to reduce the interest paid on debts. Money spent on interest could be used elsewhere in your budget.
8. You must make efforts to keep your daily living expenses as low as possible without being a hermit.
9. Cut the frills for a while and save or invest the difference.
10. Spend your money on things that historically increase in value.
11. Invest in things that will lower your risks and potential losses.
12. Invest in things that will bring in residual income.
13. Invest in things that show a trend to increase in value and demand.
14. If you are married and have two incomes, set a goal to live off one income, and bank or invest the other.

Ways to increase your income: (Be creative in keeping your expenses low)

1. Keep your daily expenses low. This will allow you to keep more of what you earn.
2. Don't pay more taxes than you are suppose to. If you normally receive a large tax refund, chances are you do not have the correct amount of deductions for withholding taxes from your paycheck (two or three times your monthly income). To keep your taxes low, you must learn and plan what deductions and credits are available to you.
3. Depending on your situation, you may consider getting a second job for a while to bring in extra income. Be sure to save this extra income, or perhaps use some of it to pay off a bill.
4. Consider a simple home-based business for diversified income as well as the tax advantages it will bring. There are businesses that require less than 15 minutes of your time daily.

YOU CAN EARN A SECOND INCOME WITHOUT A SECOND JOB

There are two tax codes in the United States; personal and business. There are very few ways of reducing your taxes if you file a personal return only. Therefore, we suggest that you own some type of business for this reason. There are many great business opportunities available; you just have to look around. However, after many years of research we suggest you take a look at an opportunity that can give you an excellent return from a small investment.

This business is affordable and simple, without the hassles of traditional businesses. This business helps everyday people like you achieve financial security with a simple, easy to use system. It offers an opportunity to make any amount of money you choose, without requiring a lot of your time. **If you are considering a business of your own as a way of increasing or replacing your income, below you will find some qualities to look for:**

Consider the following features:

1. Keep your current job
2. Enjoyment, because it compliments almost any career field
3. Growth trend, high demand product
4. Recurring income
5. Low risk
6. Viable product or service
7. Duplicable
8. Simple and Systematic
9. Perpetual
10. No employees
11. Time freedom
12. Support and ongoing training
13. Office or Home-based
14. Inflation resistant
15. Learn while you earn
16. No collections
17. Continuing education
18. No special skills
19. Low risk
20. Quick return on your investment

Wanted: People with a passion for helping others

For FREE INFORMATION, e-mail us at lawrence.surles@yahoo.com or LLsurles@yahoo.com to request this FREE INFORMATION

Ways to build your assets:

1. Contribute to your savings every time you receive any income.
2. Home ownership - If you live in it, you pay for your home, even if it is not yours. Home ownership will build equity for you and the next generation.
3. Learn to identify trends that are increasing. Even in an economic slow down, there are trends that are increasing in demand and value.
4. Buy things that traditionally increase in value.
5. Compound interest example: Lets assume that you invest $100 per month in a saving account at 8% for 10 years=$17,680, 20 years=$56,923, 30 years=$144, 028, 40 years=$337,371. These calculations do not included tax or inflation considerations.

Use the "rule of 72" to calculate your interest earnings. Divide 72 by your interest rate of return. This will show you how many years it would take for your investment to double, if you did not add any more money to your account.

CHAPTER ELEVEN
MATAINING A CREDITABLE REPUTATION

CHAPTER ELEVEN OBJECTIVES: I would like to impress upon you that having a good reputation can give you access to many opportunities that money can't. It is important to keep your reputation in top shape. In this chapter, we will share a few pointers with you. This includes your credit report. The price you pay for loans, home purchases, apartment rentals, life/auto insurance, and careers choices are affected by your credit.

Personal Creditability

- Avoid situations that could bring a bad report.
- Qualify the advice and information you receive from others.
- Maintain a life of balance: God, family, work, fun, and so on.
- When possible, make amends for your past misdeeds and misunderstandings.
- Remember- the LOVE commandment: there are none greater than this one.

How Credit Affects You:

1. It affects the amount of security deposits you make for electricity, post-paid cell phones, apartments, etc. In some cases you may not be able to lease certain apartments based on your credit worthiness.
2. The interest rate you will be charged for loans.
3. Dictates your eligibility to obtain certain loans.
4. Most insurance carriers are making changes in how they price polices, using your credit history as a factor in underwriting and rating. Your credit score can affect auto insurance rates. Your credit score is factored into a number normally called an insurance score.
5. It affects your ability to work in certain career positions.

Properly manage your credit cards to prevent overspending:

- Keep in mind that credit card debt is unsecured debt, which has a lower priority to secured debts. For example, if you had to put up any collateral, then you have a secured loan. A credit card is non-secured debt. <u>In almost every instance, you should always have a priority of paying secured debts first.</u>
- If you can't pay in full, always pay more than the minimum due, even if only one dollar extra. Minimum amounts due are often calculated to keep you in debt a long, long time.
- Stop the flood of credit card offers. Avoid the temptation for more debt.
- Negotiate for a lower interest rate at least once a year. As you pay off bills and creditors you may qualify for lower rates on the credit cards that you currently owe. Determine how many credit cards is enough for you? In most cases, retain no more than two (one for business and one for personal). Set up an emergency fund as a plan for emergencies, instead of using your credit card for emergencies. Always read the fine

print, be especially careful with introductory offers. Never co-sign for a debit or credit card. Remember, if you co-sign, the debt is yours.

- Check your credit report at least once or twice a year. Calculate your debt to credit available ratio.
- Be creative in ways you can give back to your family, community, and church. Your best gifts and talents can be worth more than you can pay with money. You can volunteer your time and skills to a worthwhile cause of your choice.
- Be sure to update your will often to assure an orderly transfer of wealth to the next generation.
- If you just can't seem to be able to quit getting into more debt, consider cutting up your credit cards until you can get your balance low enough that it can be paid in full when the bill comes in.

Hints you can use to improve your credit worthiness:

- Pay all your bills on time.
- Make extra efforts to get all past due accounts current.
- Settle and pay off outstanding debts.
- Make efforts to correct mistakes on your credit report.
- Keep the balances that you owe on your credit cards low compared to the credit limit you are allowed. Don't be hasty to close your paid off store account and major credit cards, as this could raise your balance-to-credit limit ratios.
- Only apply for credit when you need it.
- A longer credit history should help improve your credit score.
- Mixed types of credit accounts.
- If you have little or no credit history, check with local banks or credit unions about obtaining a **secured credit or debit card**. You will be asked to open a savings account, usually starting at $300 to $500. They will place your deposit on hold as security. At this point they will issue you a card with a credit limit equal to the amount on deposit. Handle it carefully, they will probably be reporting to the credit bureau. This should give you a favorable credit payment history.
- Charge only what you can afford to pay in full when the bill comes. This will help you to avoid excessive debt. Keep your balance owed to less than 10 - 20% of your credit balance available.
- If you must carry a balance, make plans to pay it off as rapidly as possible.

Things that can lower your credit score:

- Late payments
- High balance to credit limit ratio.
- Unpaid debts

Frequent reasons given by lenders when a business loan is declined

Consider giving the following reasons some attention so you can improve them as much as possible before applying for a business loan.

- Not enough collateral to satisfy loan requirements.
- A history of slow or past due payments.
- Not enough equity in the business.
- Insufficient earnings or lack of an established earnings record.

Key factors creditors use in consideration for a personal loan

1. Your current income
2. Your current financial obligations.
3. Your past credit history.
4. The amount of credit you are currently using.

Credit Reports Facts

A. No one can legally remove negative information from your credit if it is accurate.
B. Your credit report contains key information that identifies you and how you've paid your bills. Whenever you make a credit-based application, your credit report is viewed to help make a decision. That's one of the reasons that it's so important for you to check your credit report. If, for some reason, your information is reported incorrectly, it could cause you to be denied for services for which you otherwise would have been approved.
C. By Federal Law, you are entitled to a free credit report from the three major credit bureaus each year. You are also entitled to a free credit report each time you are refused credit. Credit bureaus are not government agencies, but are profit seeking businesses.
D. Debt consolidation plans can reflect negatively on your credit report.
E. You are responsible to make sure your credit report is accurate. You must not assume the credit bureaus are taking care of your reports for you.

Information that can be removed from your credit report

- *Any negative entry that does not belong to you.*

  If the information on your credit report belongs to anyone other than you, it can be removed from your credit report. Even if the information belongs to your current spouse, former spouse, or son you can't be held responsible.

- *Non verifiable information that's accurate*

  Even if the information on your credit report is accurate, if it can't be verified, then it must be removed. An example would be: If a merchant who put a negative entry on your credit report is out of business, or your records are lost, then this is grounds for removal.

- *Non verifiable that partially accurate*

  If you owe a merchant an unpaid balance of $ 6,000, but the actual amount is $9,000 and the merchant is unable to verify this with the credit bureau in the time allowed by law, it can be removed.

- *Outdated information*

   Bankruptcy entries should not be on your credit report longer than 10 years. Don't assume the credit bureaus will automatically remove it. You will probably have to request it be deleted.

General guidelines to file a credit report dispute

The, FCRA, gives you the right to dispute credit report information that is not correct. When there is information that is incorrect in your credit report, you should alert, in writing, both the credit bureau that provided the report and the information provider. If you have statements or cancelled checks that support your claim, be sure to include copies of them with your statement. Always keep the originals for your records. In your brief statement, include your name, complete address, the information you are disputing, and the reason the information is not accurate. Make copies of your credit report to send with the entries in question highlighted.

Send your credit report dispute through certified mail with return receipt requested. This way you will have proof that you sent the dispute, but also that the credit bureau received your dispute. Always keep a copy of any correspondence along with any enclosures you sent.

The Credit Bureau responses to your Dispute

By law, the credit bureau has 30 days to investigate your dispute and respond to you, in writing, with the results of the investigation. Any information you provided about the inaccuracy of the information will be forwarded to the original information provider. The information provider is then required to investigate and respond back to the credit bureau.

Once the investigation is complete, the credit bureau will provide you with the results, along with a free copy of your credit report, showing any changes made. You may also request that the credit bureau send a correction notice to any company that accessed your credit report within the past six months.

If there is inaccurate information in one credit bureau's credit report, it's likely that the information will be inaccurate on the other two bureaus' reports as well. You should check all three credit bureau reports to be sure that the information in each is complete and accurate.

- The credit reporting time limit is the maximum amount of time credit bureaus can report delinquent debts on your credit report. For most types of accounts, it's seven years from the date of delinquency. However, bankruptcies are reported for 10 years. The statute of limitations for collecting a debt is the period of time that a creditor or collector can use the court to force you to pay for a debt. Usually, the time period starts on the account's last date of activity and varies by state. The statute of limitations starts on the last date of activity on the account. Your credit report will include the account's last date of activity. Even if the statute of limitations has expired, some debt collectors will continue to attempt to collect. They're hoping you don't know about the statute of limitations and you'll pay up if they threaten you enough. They may even file a lawsuit against you. If you are certain the statute of limitations has expired, you can use that fact as justification that you do not have to pay the debt. Be careful not to restart the statute of limitations. Anytime you take an action with an account, the statute of limitations is restarted. Making a payment, making a promise of payment, entering a payment agreement, or making a charge using the account can restart your statue of limitations.

- E-mail us for the most updated information about DISPUTING INFORMATION ON YOUR CREDIT RORT - Lawrence.surles@yahoo.com

CHAPTER TWELVE

REVIEW, EVALUATE AND REVISE YOUR WRITTEN PLANS OFTEN

CHAPTER TWELVE OBJECTIVES: Review, re-evaluate, and revise your goals and plans often. We offer you access to our systematic worksheet for problem solving. If you have a situation that you would like to analyze, feel free to make a copy of this worksheet.

My problem is: _____

List things that can be done to help solve or lessen the impact of this problem below

You can use this example to help you come up with a solution to problems. Before you execute any of the things that will help you with your problem, consider the positive or negative impact of each. Put a check mark beside each step you execute. Line out any step you conclude will have negative consequences that are too risky.

These are some of the things to consider when you review, evaluate, and revise your plans:

- What is working? What is not working? What are the new challenges that need your focus? Are you running ahead or behind schedule? Are you managing by objectives, but not compromising your integrity?

Review this checklist regularly: Evaluate your progress. Please answer true or false. (Hopefully you will be able to answer "true" to all of these in the long run). Each statement or question will have reference to your activities in the last 12 months, unless otherwise stated.

1. _____ My property taxes are up to date.
2. _____ I have at least six times or more of my monthly income.
3. _____ I have a savings account.
4. _____ I am not nearing the credit limit on at least one of my credit cards.
5. _____ I can pay all my bills if my spouse lost their job.
6. _____ I believe my financial situation has improved.
7. _____ I paid less than $100 in interest this year.
8. _____ I have not paid late fees of any kind in the last 12 months.
9. _____ I have reviewed a copy of my (3) credit reports.

10. _____ I have not been disapproved for credit in the last 12 months.
11. _____ I have health insurance.
12. _____ I have a valid will.
13. _____ I have life insurance or adequate assets to settle my estate.
14. _____ I have a checking account.
15. _____ I own less than three personal credit cards.
16. _____ I have paid more than the minimum due on my credit accounts.
17. _____ I have not written postdated checks for any reason.
18. _____ I do not have sad thoughts about my debts.
19. _____ I do not use "pay day lending" companies to borrow money.
20. _____ I do not have debts on which I don't make payments.
21. _____ Most of the time my paycheck covers my bills.
22. _____ I saved a portion of my last paycheck.
23. _____ I have at least $1,000 in liquid savings.
24. _____ I did not borrow money for my last vacation.
25. _____ I have not paid late fees within the last 12 months.
26. _____ I have not received collection calls within the last 12 months.
27. _____ I do not expect to live on my social security income alone.
28. _____ I did not pay a minimum balance fee for maintaining a low account balance.
29. _____ I paid all of my credit card charges in full.
30. _____ I am not too proud to ask for help if I need it.
31. _____ I seek to have balance in my life: recreation, work, family, etc.
32. _____ If I was to buy a car, I would try to pay it off in 36 months or less.
33. _____ I do not owe debts of more than one years salary, excluding mortgage.
34. _____ I have at least two months salary saved.
35. _____ I have at least six months salary saved.
36. _____ My last tax refund was less than one month of my gross income.
37. _____ I have a written monthly budget.
38. _____ I look for honest ways to pay less tax.
39. _____ I look for honest ways to reduce my expenses.
40. _____ I look for ways to work less and earn more.
41. _____ I have updated my balance sheet within the last 12 months.
42. _____ I have an automatic savings plan (draft or payroll deduction).
43. _____ I have updated my net-worth sheet within the last 12 months.
44. _____ I have reviewed my goals list and deleted the one I wish not to pursue.
45. _____ I have reviewed my goals list, and added goals that are important to me.
46. _____ The administrator of my estate knows where my important papers are located.
47. _____ Credit cards can be an important tool that can be used to help improve your credit.
49. _____ Stock market investing is not a guarantee of earning.
50. _____ Creating a written plan of action is an important step in financial and career management.
51 _____ Bankruptcy should not be your first option to help you get rid of debt.

52. _____ According to the IRS and tax experts, making charitable contributions will normally lower your taxable rate.

53. _____ Having an emergency fund can help you avoid adding new debt when you have an emergency, causing you fall back into a deficit spending pattern.

Total survey points earned from each chapter

Chapter1,2, 3, 4,5,6,7,8,9,10,11,12
Enter your total here

Things you can do to discourage use of your credit card.

1. Maintain an adequate savings account. (At one month gross salary).
2. Pay cash as much as possible.
3. Purpose to pay all credit cards in full each time your bill arrives.
4. Leave your credit cards at home when you are near home.
5. If you can't seem to stop charging, cut up your credit card, but don't cancel the account yet.

Strategies that can be used to pay off your credit card debt

- It is almost never a good idea to use your savings, or 401k, to payoff credit card debt.
- Start paying on the card with the next highest interest rate, if you have a positive cash flow.
- Focusing on one card at a time gives you clear financial goals, and minimizes your interest expense. You should be paying as much as possible on this card, while paying at no more than $1.00 above the minimums on the remainder.
- If available, you can use a home equity loan to pay off credit card debt. The interest on home equity loans is typically lower than credit card rates and is usually tax deductible. This can be an effective repayment method if you can handle it with discipline. You run the risk of paying down the home equity loan at the same time you're running up more debt on your newly cleared credit cards. Remember, your home equity loan, will be secured by a lien on your home. If for any reason you can't make your payments, you'll be in default, and the lender can foreclose on your home.
- Another way to pay off your credit card debt is to transfer your balances to lower-rate credit card accounts. It should allow you to reduce interest fees and pay more against your principal balance.
- It's always best to control new spending and pay more than the required minimum payment whenever possible. When you make minimum payments, they cover little more than the finance charges. You will continue to carry the bulk of your balance

forward for many years without actually reducing that balance. Charging only what you can afford to pay off each month gives you the best benefits of a credit card.

- Do not use your credit card for routine purchases, unless you are getting a substantial discount. Purchases such as gas, groceries, and entertainment should be made with cash or the equivalent. Using your credit card for routine purchases that you can't pay in full when the bill comes is sure-fire way to spiral into debt. Other examples are: DVD's, contributions at church, eating out, and gifts for others.

Negotiating Debts

- Never accept the collector's first or second offer to a settlement.
- Make sure you get every agreement in writing.
- You may have greater leverage with the help of a credit counseling service. They can help you reduce interest charges, waive fees, etc.
- Remember, if you make a promise of payment or payment, your statue of limitations on your debt may start over.
- Your creditors would rather get some money from you rather than no money at all. Let your creditors know you are having financial difficulty. Express your willingness to pay the debt and ask if they can help ease the burden by lowering your monthly payment or decreasing your interest rate (or both). Many credit card companies and banks have hardship programs intended for this type of situation. Don't be afraid to ask.
- If you're struggling with debt, don't wait too long before asking for professional help. If you don't have the time or know-how to get positive results on your own, considering turning to a good credit counseling company. Once you're in debt and you're in a position where you can't save, it's almost impossible to get out from it. A consultation with a good credit counselor usually takes an hour or two, but well worth the time. Good credit counseling agencies construct an individualized budget and repayment plan for free, or a low cost.

Entries that can be found on your credit report

1. A Charge-off

A charge-off is one of the worst entries that can appear on your credit report. Creditors typically charge off seriously delinquent accounts that have not been paid on time for six months straight. They usually remain on your report for seven years. Your creditor will normally report a charged-off account status to the credit bureaus. This status will normally remain on your credit report for seven years from the date you first went delinquent. Your credit score will normally drop after a charge-off. As time passes, your credit score can improve if no additional negative entries are placed in your credit report.

2. Bankruptcy

Filing bankruptcy allows you to legally remove liability for some or all of your debts, depending on the type of bankruptcy you file. Your credit report will reflect each of the accounts you included in your bankruptcy. Even though the bankruptcy information will remain on your credit report for seven to 10 years, you can sometimes begin rebuilding your credit soon after your debts have been discharged. There are two types of personal bankruptcies: Chapter 7 and Chapter 13. They usually do not wipe out child support, alimony, fines, taxes, and some student loan obligations.

3. Foreclosure

If you default on your mortgage loan, your lender will repossess your home and auction it off to recover the amount of the mortgage. When your home is foreclosed it can severely damage your credit, and limiting your ability to obtain new credit in the future. A foreclosure will remain on your credit report for seven years.

4. Tax liens

When you don't pay property taxes on your home or another piece of property, the government can seize the property and auction it off for the unpaid taxes. Even if your home is foreclosed because of a tax lien, you are still responsible for the mortgage loan. Non-payment of the mortgage will also hurt your credit. Unpaid tax liens remain on your credit report for 15 years, while paid tax liens may remain for 10 years.

5. Lawsuits or judgments

Some creditors may take you to court and sue you for a debt, if other collections fail. If the lawsuit is accurate and a judgment is entered against you, it can remain on your credit report for 7 years from the date of filing, even after you satisfy the judgment.

Preventative Steps to Avoid Foreclosure

- **Save a portion of your income regularly.** Put away some money each month to have an emergency fund in case something unexpected happens, such as losing your job or other cutbacks.

- **Reduce expenses.** Think about ways you can save money; for instance, temporarily canceling cable, magazine, and gym memberships. By cutting back to the bare necessities, you may be able to cut your expense even more. Remember – every little bit helps. Question every expense, even your charitable donations.

- **Call your lender.** This is the single most important thing you can do. Lenders want borrowers, not properties – they would prefer to see you keep your home. **Most will work with you while you get back on your feet, especially in a down economy.**

- **Be honest with your lender.** Different situations require different solutions. It will matter to your lender to know if your financial problems are temporary, for example, due to an injury that puts you out of work for a few months, or are more long term, such as a cut in pay or a layoff.

- **Make sure secured debts such as your home get priority consideration.** Have a clear picture of what your debts are and make your mortgage the top priority.

In most cases, pay the mortgage, even if you don't have money left over for food. Debt collectors can be very aggressive. Therefore, if you can't pay all your debts, make sure your home is protected from foreclosure by paying your mortgage and other notes secured by your home.

- **Contact a non-profit housing counseling agency.** Don't try to handle things alone. This non-profit can give you valuable advice. The HOPE National helpline, 1-888-995-HOPE, is dedicated to helping homeowners facing foreclosure 24 hours every day. Spanish speaking counselors are also available. This non-profit housing counseling agency may be able to help you restructure your bills so that you have an easier time paying them. They can help you create a budget that suits your specific needs.

You know you need help from a credit counselor when ...

- You can't save regularly.
- Creditors are calling and you don't have the money to pay.
- You are going to lose your job.
- You are not current on your home loan.

Rebuilding your bad credit

One of the most effective methods for repairing credit is having a good payment history. If you already have a mortgage or credit cards, you should keep making timely payments and reducing those balances. This will strengthen your credit as your credit balances decrease. If you have the need; you may want to apply for a post-paid cell phone. You may be asked to pay a deposit, but it will help put good marks on your credit report.

A secured card is an option. If you have trouble qualifying for a credit card, you may opt to apply for a secured card. These cards have credit limits based on a required deposit made by you into a savings account. You use the card just as you would any other credit card.

If denied credit, ask why. Ask any creditor that denies you credit to give you the reasons you were denied. Reasons may include income, employment or credit history. It is important to find out why you are denied, because frequent inquiries (applying for credit) on your credit report can be viewed as a negative to a potential creditor. If you are denied credit, you can request a free copy of your credit report to see if there is erroneous data on it and have corrections made.

Using home equity loans to improve credit. These loans are relatively inexpensive compared to other types of loans, and they may offer a tax deduction for the interest portion of the loan. The downside is that the collateral for the loan is the house, and they've gotten much harder to get. **Although risky, a home equity loan can be an extremely useful strategy if it's used properly.** But people need understand the implications and risk involved. The other disadvantage is the low-pressure repayment terms. Your new monthly payment should be at least as large as your previous monthly payment, if you want to really make progress. If you can pay more, you should, because you'll pay it off faster.

Credit Cards. Using your credit card to consolidate debts is risky, but it can be done successfully. Only transfer debts to your card if the interest rate on this card will be less than the rate you are paying on the other loans. Make sure you will have a fix rate for the life of the loan.

One of the best ways to assess the condition of your finances is by pulling your credit reports. This can be accomplished a couple of ways.

1. Go to annualcreditreport.com, which is the only authorized source for consumers to access their annual credit report online for free.
2. Call 1 (877) 322-8228.

Basic tax lessons that can benefit you

1. Your tax refund check may be too big

If you repeatedly get a large tax refund, you are probably over-withholding. You may not be getting the best use of your money. In reality, you are giving the government an interest free loan. Refunds of this type occur because individuals have too much payroll tax taken out of their pay check. You can change this by completing a Form W-4 with your employer. Keep in mind that you are able to adjust your W-4 at any time to prevent a short fall, or from withholding too much.

2. Not claiming enough exemptions

If you end up paying taxes at the end of the year, you may be under-withholding. As you did to correct over-withholding, adjust the amount of taxes taken from your check to ensure that you pay enough. Extra withholding may be needed to help cover taxes on that money so that you don't have to come up with quarterly estimated tax payments.

3. You are taxed at different rates according to your bracket of income

The income tax system in the United States is a progressive tax system, which means you pay more than one tax rate on your income. Progressive tax means the more you earn, the more you pay.

4. Itemizing isn't always necessary

There are several ways to get your final tax bill as small as possible. The most common way is through deductions, either the standard amount or itemized expenses. But there are some tax breaks you can claim without having to itemize. They are adjustments to your income and are items you can claim to arrive at your adjusted gross income. Talk to the IRS, your financial advisor, or tax preparer.

5. Tax deductions have their limitations

Deductions are a valuable tax-reduction method, many have limits. Even if you do itemize, some deductions must meet a criteria before they help you. For example, only medical expenses that exceed a certain percent of your adjusted gross income can be deducted. Being aware of deductibility limits can help you establish a tax strategy to get around them. If you own a business, this will also plan expenditures in a way that will help ease your tax burden at the end of the year.

6. All income is not taxed the same

In addition to the regular tax brackets, your income is taxed differently depending on how you earn it. The IRS generally classifies income as earned or unearned. Generally, as a rule of thumb, earned income is that it which comes from a business activity or job. Unearned income typically comes from investment sources, inheritances or other passive activities, such as rents from property you own. Much of unearned income is taxed at different rates than ordinary income. Generally you pay lower rates on capital gains and dividends you receive. Consult your tax preparer or other competent authority to make sure you are not closing other tax advantages. You have to have earned income to make an IRA contribution.

Frequently Asked Questions & Answers

What is a secured credit card? It is a special type of credit card that requires you to deposit a certain amount with the issuing institution. The credit that you are granted is normally a percentage of the deposited amount. In most cases, the institution will report your use of the card to the credit bureau. This can be useful in establishing credit for the first time, or to rebuild credit. Be sure to inquire as to whether they will be reporting your account activities to the credit bureaus.

What is a discount broker? It is a broker that normally charges lower fees than a full service broker. In most cases you will have to research and wisely choose your own investments.

How long does negative information stay on my credit report? According to the Fair Credit Reporting Act (FCRA), most negative information will stay on your credit report for a minimum of seven years. There are exceptions for certain types of negative information.

- Delinquency information like late payments and collections remain on your report for seven years from the date of delinquency.
- **Charge off**- seven years + 180 days from the date reported to the credit bureau.
- **Student loans** -seven years.
- **Bankruptcy** – 10 years from the date you file.
- **Foreclosures**- seven years.
- Law suits or judgments-seven years from the date of filing.
- **Paid tax liens**- seven years from the date paid.
- **Unpaid tax liens**-15 years.

What is discretionary income? This is the amount you have for spending after all your financial obligations have been met.

What is foreclosure? In the contract you signed when your mortgage lender loaned you money to buy your house, you agreed that if you can't repay the loan, the lender can reclaim ownership of the house. If you do not pay your monthly mortgage payment, you are technically in default on your mortgage. State laws vary, but generally, a loan that is as little as 90 days delinquent can be considered in foreclosure.

What is CD laddering? It is the staggering, or spreading of CD's so they will mature on different dates. For example, depositing new CDs every six months to a year will allow you to take advantage of rate changes. The idea is to have liquid money available at various times during year. This way you can take advantage of any rate increases.

What is credit utilization? The amount of purchasing power that you have is calculated as the total credit available, divided by your total debts. Credit utilization is 30% of your credit score and is expressed as a percentage. Higher credit utilizations result in lower credit scores. Example: credit available = $2,000, total debt = $1,000, credit utilization = **50%**

(Your debt to credit ratio).

What is a closed-end account? It is an account that you can't add any more debt to. A credit card is not a closed-end account.

How can I attend one of your workshops? E-mail us at *llsurles@yahoo.com* or *Lawrence.surles@yahoo.com*.